LEARNING RABBITMQ WITH C#

SAINESHWAR BAGERI

FIRST EDITION 2018

Copyright © BPB Publications, INDIA

ISBN: 978-93-88176-94-1

All Rights Reserved. No part of this publication can be stored in a retrieval system or reproduced in any form or by any means without the prior written permission of the publishers.

LIMITS OF LIABILITY AND DISCLAIMER OF WARRANTY

The Author and Publisher of this book have tried their best to ensure that the programmes, procedures and functions described in the book are correct. However, the author and the publishers make no warranty of any kind, expressed or implied, with regard to these programmes or the documentation contained in the book. The author and publisher shall not be liable in any event of any damages, incidental or consequential, in connection with, or arising out of the furnishing, performance or use of these programmes, procedures and functions. Product name mentioned are used for identification purposes only and may be trademarks of their respective companies.

All trademarks referred to in the book are acknowledged as properties of their respective owners.

Distributors:

BPB PUBLICATIONS
20, Ansari Road, Darya Ganj
New Delhi-110002
Ph: 23254990/23254991

BPB BOOK CENTRE
376 Old Lajpat Rai Market,
Delhi-110006
Ph: 23861747

DECCAN AGENCIES
4-3-329, Bank Street,
Hyderabad-500195
Ph: 24756967/24756400

MICRO MEDIA
Shop No. 5, Mahendra Chambers, 150
DN Rd. Next to Capital Cinema, V.T.
(C.S.T.) Station, MUMBAI-400 001 Ph:
22078296/22078297

Published by Manish Jain for BPB Publications, 20, Ansari Road, Darya Ganj, New Delhi-110002 and Printed by Repro India Ltd., Mumbai

Table of Contents

Preface vii
Acknowledgements ix
    RabbitMQ Introduction 1
-     What is RabbitMQ? 1
-     Why and when should we use RabbitMQ? 1
    What is AMQP? 1
    RabbitMQ Setup 3
-     What is Erlang 3
    Installing Erlang 4
    Downloading RabbitMQ 4
    Installing RabbitMQ 5
    Starting RabbitMQ Server 5
    RabbitMQ Exchanges 9
-     What are the Exchanges? 9
    Adding Exchanges 12
    RabbitMQ Queues 15
-     What is the Queue? 15
    Parameters of Queues in Details 15
    Adding Queue 20
    Binding in RabbitMQ 22
-     What is Binding 22
    RabbitMQ Users 24
-     Currently Supported by the Management Plugin 25
    Creating Users 25
    Setting Privilege to Access Virtual Hosts 26
    RabbitMQ Virtual Hosts 29
-     What are Virtual Hosts? 29
    Creating Users 31
    Setting Privilege to Access Virtual Hosts 31
    Connections 34
-     **Channels** 36
-     Note for Mode 36
    Note for Prefetch count 36

- **Publishing Message** 38
  - Snapshot after Publishing Message 39
- **Reading Message** 40
  - Snapshot while Reading the Message 41
- **Delete Message** 42
- **Publish Message Using C# to RabbitMQ** 44
  - Creating RequestRabbitMQ Application 44
  - Adding RabbitMQ.Client NuGet Package 44
  - Adding Direct Exchange 44
  - Adding Queue 46
  - Binding the Demoqueue with demoExchange 48
  - Adding a Directmessages Class 50
  - Consume Message Using C# to RabbitMQ 52
  - Adding RabbitMQ.Client NuGet Package 53
  - Code snippet of MessageReceiver class 53
  - Queue is Empty 56
  - Queue after Publishing Message 56
- **Using RabbitMQ Direct Message Exchanges with .Net Application** 57
  - Types of Exchanges 57
  - Creating RequestRabbitMQ Application 57
  - Adding RabbitMQ.Client NuGet Package 58
  - Adding Direct Exchange 58
  - Adding Queue 59
  - Binding the request.queue with request.exchange 59
  - Adding a Directmessages Class 59
  - Now Let's See queue status request.queue 61
  - Creating RabbitMQConsumer Application 62
  - Adding RabbitMQ.Client NuGet Package 62
  - Queue after publishing Message 66
  - Conclusion 66
- **Using RabbitMQ Topic Message Exchanges with .Net Application** 67
  - What is the Topic Exchange? 67
  - Creating RequestRabbitMQ Application 67
  - Adding RabbitMQ.Client NuGet Package 68
  - Adding Topic Exchange 68
  - Adding Queue 68
  - Binding the topic.delhi.queue with topic.exchange 70

Adding a Topicmessages Class 70
Published Message to "topic.bombay.queue" 72
Creating RabbitMQConsumer Application 72
Adding RabbitMQ.Client NuGet Package 73
The queue has one Request which we have published 75
Published Message to topic.delhi.queue 76
Published Message to "topic.delhi.queue" 77
Consumed Message from topic.delhi.queue 79
Conclusion 79

- **Using RabbitMQ Fanout Message Exchanges with .Net Application 80**
  What is a Fanout Exchange? 80
  Adding RabbitMQ.Client NuGet Package 81
  Adding Fanout Exchange 81
  Adding Queue 81
  Adding a Fanoutmessages Class 83
  Published Message to all queues of "fanout.exchange" 85
  Creating RabbitMQConsumer Application 85
  Adding RabbitMQ.Client NuGet Package 86
  Conclusion 91

- **Using RabbitMQ Headers Message Exchanges with .Net Application .. 92**
  What is a Headers exchange? 92
  Creating RequestRabbitMQ Application 92
  Adding RabbitMQ.Client NuGet Package 93
  Adding Fanout Exchange 93
  Binding the Queues 94
  Adding a Headersmessages Class 96
  Creating RabbitMQConsumer Application 98
  Adding RabbitMQ.Client NuGet Package 98
  The queue has one request which we have published 101
  Conclusion 102

Preface

Learn Rabbitmq with C# is meant for developers, architects, solution providers, consultants, and engineers to develop solutions using RabbitMQ message queueing with.Net Applications.

RabbitMQ is an open source and cross-platform message broker which Implements AMQP protocol and is lightweight and easy to deploy on-premises or in the cloud. It is built on Erlang which is also used by WhatsApp for messaging.RabbitMQ provides a way to exchange data between applications such as a message sent a Node.js application, or Java application can read the from.Net application.

In a fast-paced world where the applications need to provide fast responses to the end user, we develop Bussiness Web applications in the form of portals and also use same to send Emails, Messages, Notifications to ends Users slowing down the performance of the application. Using Rabbitmq, we can remove this burden from the Portal by using Exchanges and Queues for handling Messages and Notifications.

RabbitMQ is a Magical Tool for the IT world.

Acknowledgements

I'd like to thank the following people:

To my parents for supporting and encouraging me.

To Manish Jain for providing me with the opportunity to write this book.

To Shivprasad Koirala and Sukesh Marla for supporting and encouraging me to write this book.

And to all the other people who played a role in getting this book ready. Thanks for your
hard work!

RabbitMQ Introduction

What is RabbitMQ?

RabbitMQ is an AMQP message broker, it is the most popular open source and cross-platform message broker.

It is built on Erlang which is also used by WhatsApp for messaging.

RabbitMQ is also a way to exchange data between applications such as a message sent from .Net application can be read by a Node.js application or Java application.

RabbitMQ is lightweight and easy to deploy on premises and in the cloud. It supports multiple messaging protocols. RabbitMQ can be deployed in distributed and federated configurations to meet high-scale, high-availability requirements.

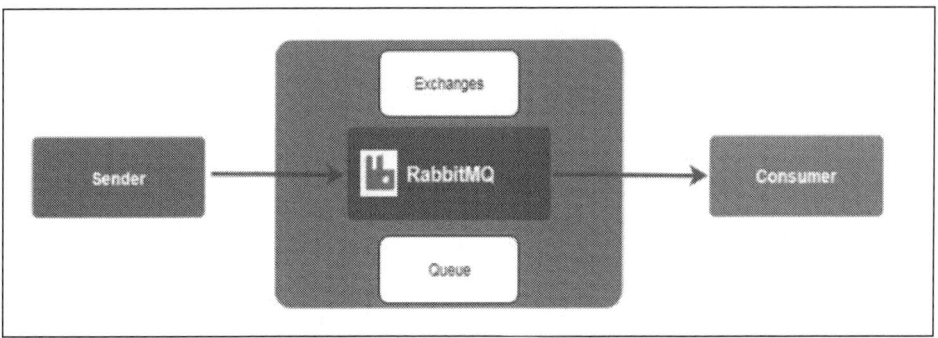

Why and when should we use RabbitMQ?

We should use RabbitMQ because it is open source and easy to use with many languages such as .Net, Java, Python, Ruby, Node Js.

We can use RabbitMQ to remove some heavy work from our web application such as sending Reports in Emails, in Excel or Pdf format's or sending email, SMS or another task such as a trigger to some other applications to start processing.

Nowadays most people do all this task into single application sending emails or SMS, reports which bit heavy task which is also handled by IIS if you separate this task then IIS will get more space (memory) to serve more request.

After understanding a bit about RabbitMQ next we are going to Install Erlang and RabbitMQ on Windows.

What is AMQP?
The **Advanced Message Queuing Protocol (AMQP)** is an open standard application layer protocol for message-oriented, the defining features of AMQP are message orientation, queuing, routing (including point-to-point and publish-and-subscribe), reliability and security.

It was developed by JPMorgan and iMatix Corporation.

Key Features

AMQP was designed with the following main characteristics as goals:
- Security
- Reliability
- Interoperability
- Standard
- Open

Various Client Libraries

RabbitMQ support various number of operating systems and various language and it has various clients for different languages such as:

1. .Net
2. Java
3. Spring Framework
4. Ruby
5. Python
6. PHP
7. Objective-C and Swift
8. JavaScript
9. GO
10. Perl

RabbitMQ Setup

In this part, we are going to learn how to setup RabbitMQ step by step:
1. What is Erlang
2. Downloading Erlang
3. Installing Erlang
4. Downloading RabbitMQ
5. Installing RabbitMQ
6. Starting RabbitMQ Server
7. Enabling web management plugin
8. Web Management plugin
9. Conclusion

What is Erlang

Erlang is a general-purpose programming language and runtime environment. Erlang has built-in support for concurrency, distribution, and fault tolerance. Erlang is used in several large telecommunication systems from Ericsson.
Referred from: http://erlang.org/faq/introduction.html

Link to download Erlang

http://www.erlang.org/downloads

Installing Erlang

In this part, just click on Erlang setup which you have downloaded to install.

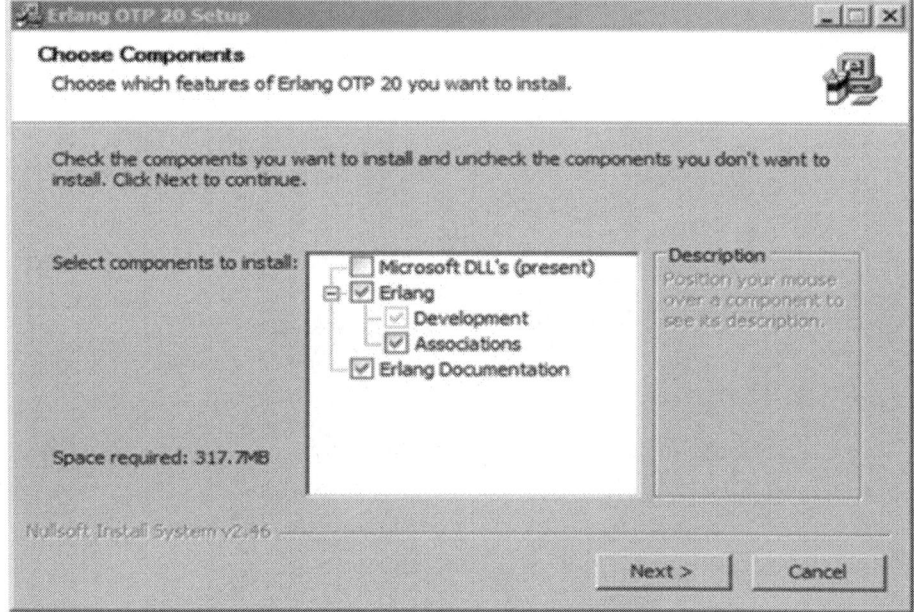

After downloading Erlang setup, just install it, after installing we are going to download RabbitMQ.

Downloading RabbitMQ

First, we are going to download RabbitMQ setup for windows from link: https://www.rabbitmq.com/download.html

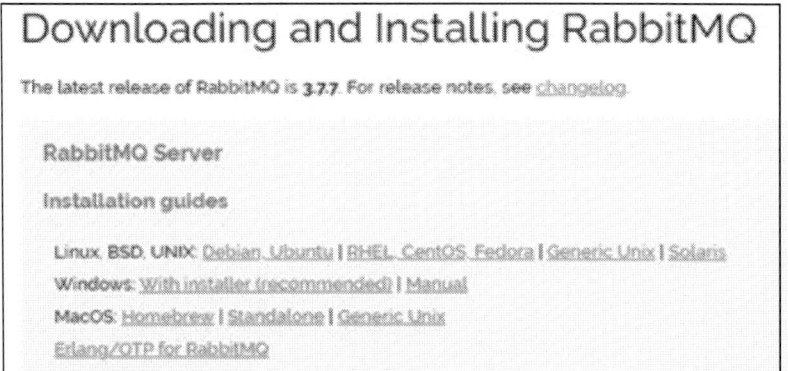

After downloading RabbitMQ, now we are going to Install RabbitMQ.

Installing RabbitMQ

In this part just click on RabbitMQ setup which you have downloaded to install.

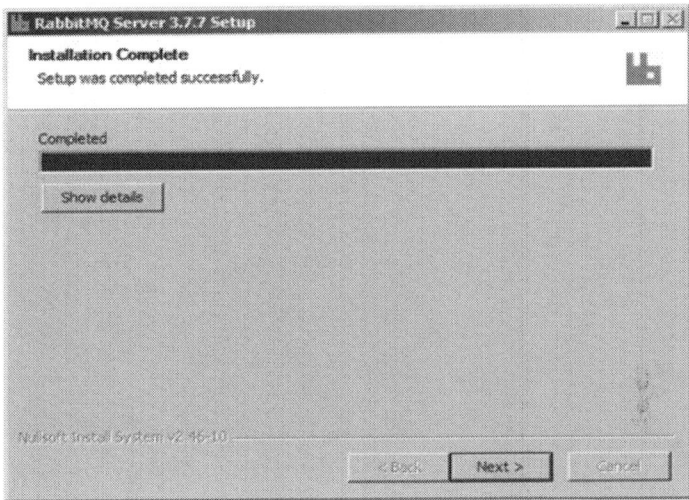

After installing Rabbit MQ, search RabbitMQ command prompt and open it with admin privilege.

Starting RabbitMQ Server

In this part we are going to open **RabbitMQ Command Prompt** with admin privileges for checking status of RabbitMQ server.

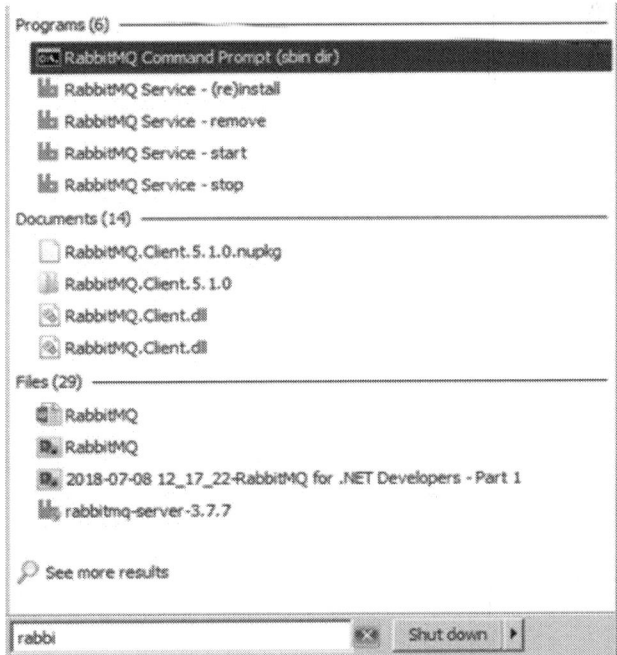

After opening command prompt, enter command **"rabbitmqctl status"** for checking status of RabbitMQ server. If it shows you an error as below snapshot then you need to follow some step given as follows:.

```
Administrator: RabbitMQ Command Prompt (sbin dir)

C:\Program Files\RabbitMQ Server\rabbitmq_server-3.7.7\sbin>rabbitmqctl status
Status of node rabbit@Sai-PC ...
Error: unable to perform an operation on node 'rabbit@Sai-PC'. Please see diagno
stics information and suggestions below.

Most common reasons for this are:

 * Target node is unreachable (e.g. due to hostname resolution, TCP connection o
r firewall issues)
 * CLI tool fails to authenticate with the server (e.g. due to CLI tool's Erlang
 cookie not matching that of the server)
 * Target node is not running

In addition to the diagnostics info below:

 * See the CLI, clustering and networking guides on http://rabbitmq.com/document
ation.html to learn more
 * Consult server logs on node rabbit@Sai-PC

DIAGNOSTICS
===========

attempted to contact: ['rabbit@Sai-PC']
```

Steps, if you get Error (Authentication failed (rejected by the remote node), check the Erlang cookie)

1. In File Explorer, navigate to your user directory. (Paste %userprofile% in the address bar)
2. If you already have the file .erlang.cookie in there, delete it. If not, just go to the next step.
3. In a second File Explorer, navigate to C:\Windows\System32\config\systemprofile.
4. Find the file .erlang.cookie and copy it to your user directory.
5. Now your rabbitmqctl should be able to authenticate.

Links for solution

- https://stackoverflow.com/questions/47893899/authentication-failed-rejected-by-the-remote-node-please-check-the-erlang-coo?rq=1
- https://stackoverflow.com/questions/28258392/rabbitmq-has-nodedown-error

After you completed steps, again if you are running the same command **"rabbitmqctl status"** then the following screen should appear.

Now we have started server, next we are going to enable web management plugin of RabbitMQ.

Enabling web management plugin

For enabling web management plugin, you need to start RabbitMQ command prompt with administrator privilege and enter the command **rabbitmq-plugins enable rabbitmq_management**.

After executing this command, you will see following plugins will be enabled.

This screen is same but I have already enabled plugin that's why it is showing different messages

Now you can open web management plugin in the browser.

Web Management plugin

Now to use web management plugin, enter localhost URL in browser http://localhost:15672/.

After entering localhost URL in browser, it will ask for credentials for accessing web management plugin.

The default **Username** and **Password** of management plugin is **guest** (Username: "guest" | Password: "guest").

After login with default credentials, below overview screen will appear.

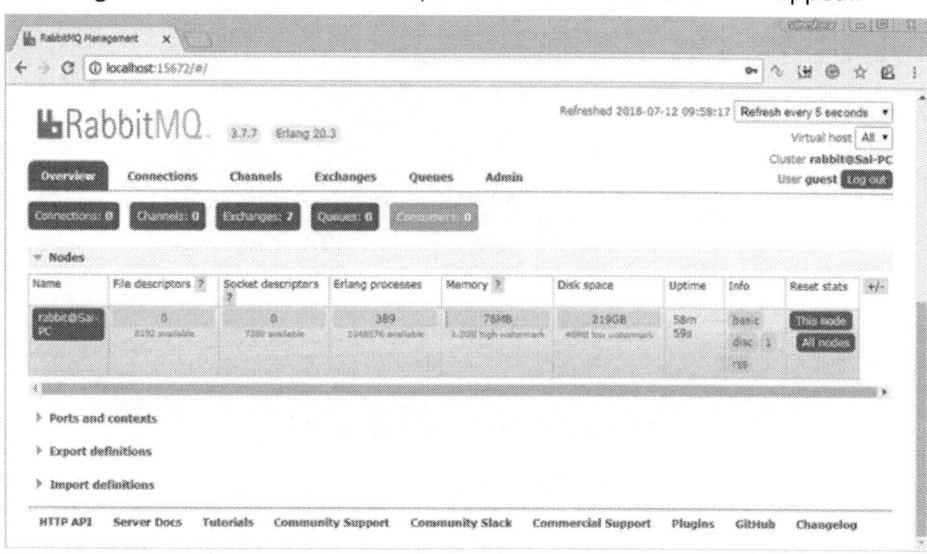

For detail information on all tabs, you can visit: https://www.cloudamqp.com/blog/2015-05-27-part3-rabbitmq-for-beginners_the-management-interface.html#overview

RabbitMQ Exchanges

What are the Exchanges?

When a producer creates a message, it is not directly sent to a queue, first message is send to exchanges after that a routing agent reads and sends it to the appropriate queue with the help of header attributes, bindings, and routing keys. There are four types of exchanges which route the message in different ways along with that, there are various parameters which you can set such as Type, Durability Auto-delete, Internal.

Direct Exchange

Direct: A direct exchange delivers messages to queues based on a message routing key. In a direct exchange, the message is routed to the queues whose binding key exactly matches the routing key of the message.

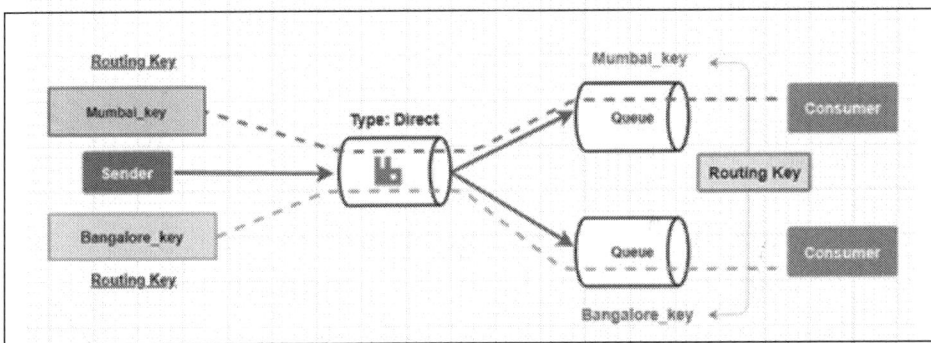

Fanout Exchange

Fanout: A fanout exchange routes messages to all of the queues that are bound to it.

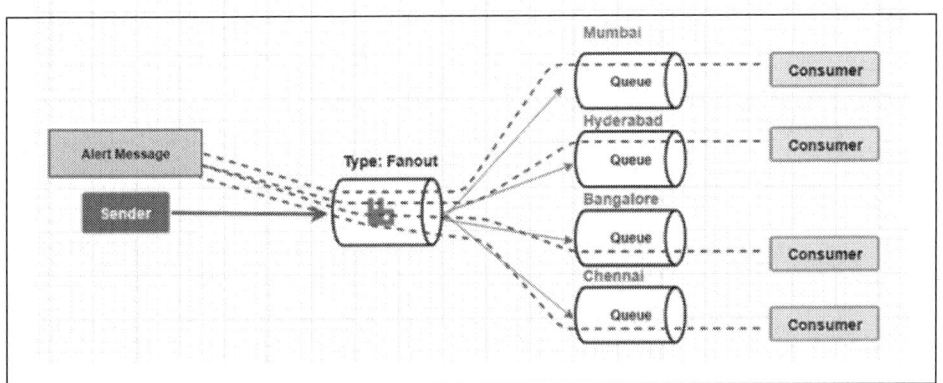

Topic Exchange

Topic: The topic exchange does a wildcard match between the routing key and the routing pattern specified in the binding.

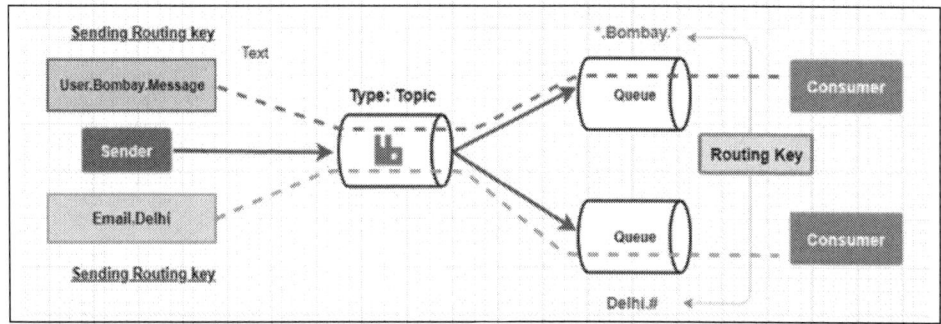

Headers Exchange

Headers: Headers exchanges use the message header attributes for routing.

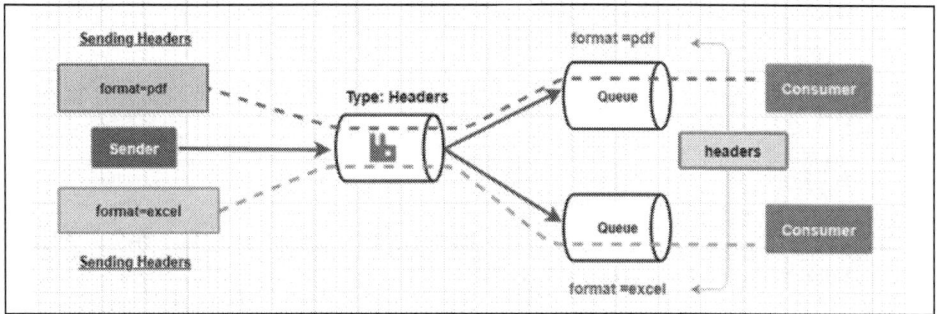

Properties Details

Name

The name will be an exchange name which you will set, it must be unique.

Type

Direct: A direct exchange delivers messages to queues based on a message routing key. In a direct exchange, the message is routed to the queues whose binding key exactly matches the routing key of the message.

Fanout: A fanout exchange routes messages to all of the queues that are bound to it.

Topic: The topic exchange does a wildcard match between the routing key and the routing pattern specified in the binding.

Headers: Headers exchanges use the message header attributes for routing.

Durability

Durability is a property of exchange which tells that a message can survive server restarts (broker restart).

There are two types of durability options:

1. Durable
2. Transient (Non-Durable)
1. **Durable**: if you mark exchange as durable then it will survive server restarts.
2. **Transient**: if you mark exchange as Transient then it will not survive server restarts.

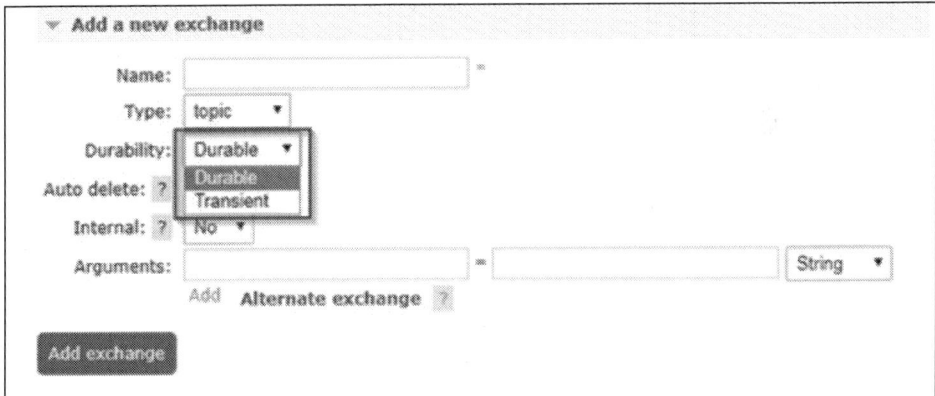

Auto delete

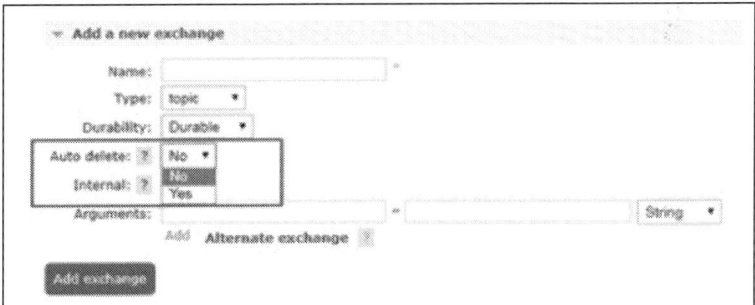

There are two options in auto delete.

1. Yes
2. No

If yes, the exchange will delete itself after at least one queue or exchange has been bound to this one, and then all queues or exchanges have been unbound.

E.g. In this part, if you create an exchange and bind it to a queue and as you unbind queue it will delete it's exchange also.

Internal

If set, the exchange may not be used directly by publishers, but only when bound to other exchanges. Internal exchanges are used to construct wiring that is not visible to applications.

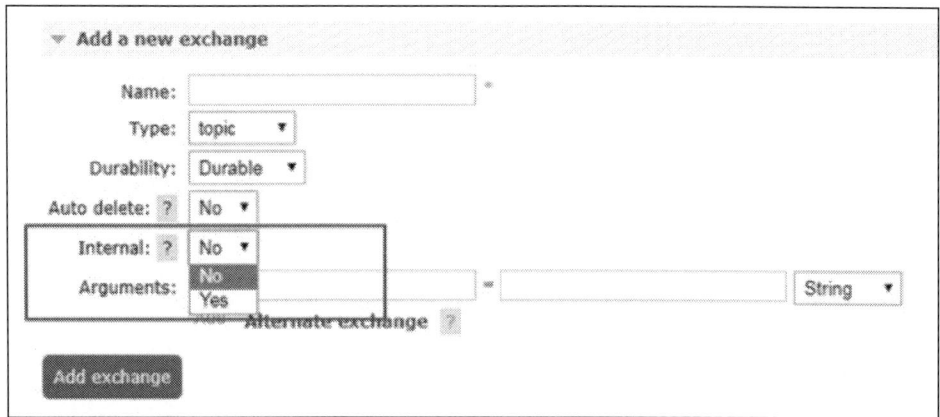

Alternate-exchange

If there is an issue in publishing message to an exchange you can specify alternate exchange it will send a message to another queue.

Adding Exchanges

To add exchanges, we are first going to log in with default credentials and then we are going to choose Exchanges tab.

Learning RabbitMQ With C#   **13**

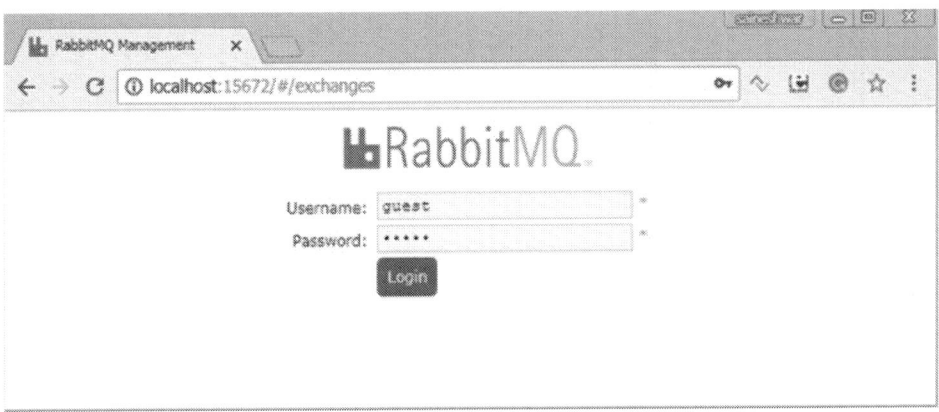

After choosing tab you will see *"Add a new exchange panel"* just click on that panel to expand, next after expansion it will ask for exchange name for demo we are going to name exchange as **"demoexchange"** and in type we are going to choose *"direct"* and click on the add button to create.

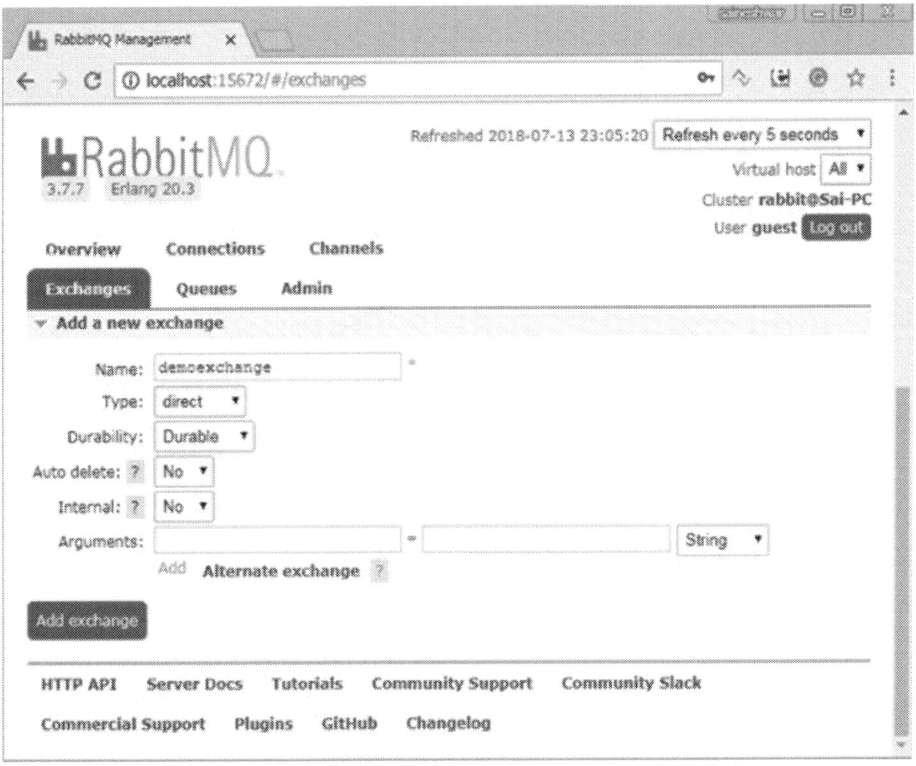

After entering all details, we are going to click on **Add exchange** button to create an exchange. **Snapshot after adding Exchanges**

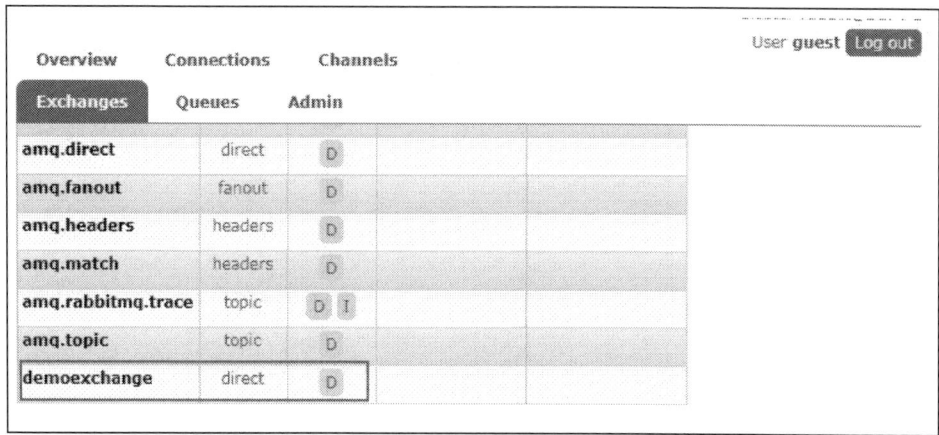

In a similar way, we can add various exchanges and with different types.
Snapshot after adding Exchanges

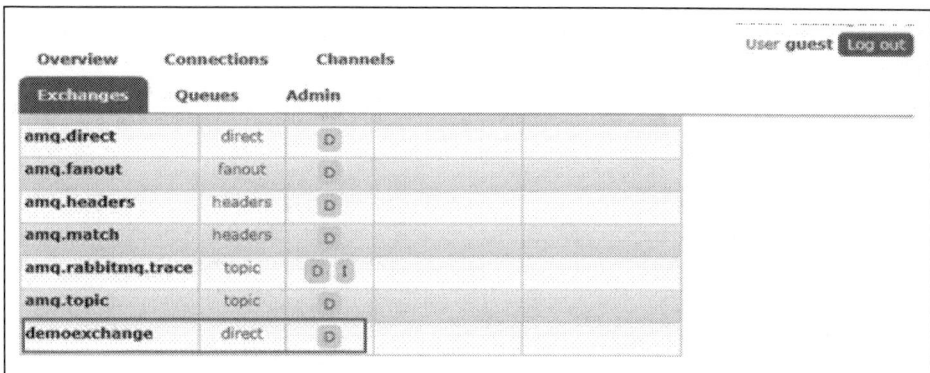

In a similar way, we can add various exchanges and with different types.

RabbitMQ Queues

What is the Queue?

A Queue is a Buffer that stores messages that are sent from exchanges to queues.

Parameters of Queues in Details

Name:

Name of the queue which we can reference in the application. The name must be unique and it must not be any system defined queue name.

Durability:

Durability is a property of queue which tells that a message can survive server restarts (broker restart).

There are two types of durability options:

1. Durable
2. Transient (Non-Durable)
1. **Durable**: If you mark queue as durable then it will survive server restarts.
2. **Transient**: If you mark exchange as Transient then it will not survive server restarts.

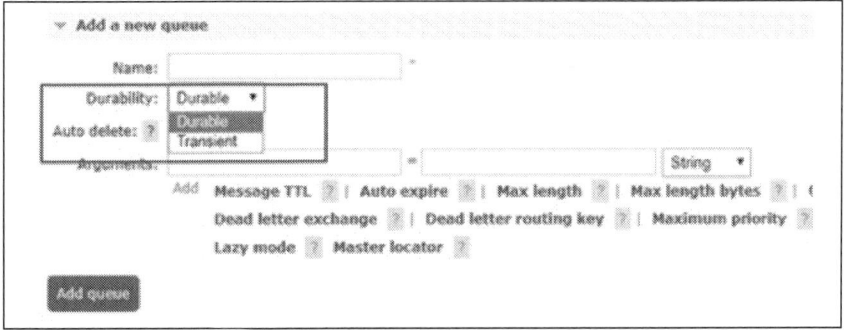

Auto delete

There are two options in auto delete:
1. Yes
2. No

If the queue is exclusive, the durability attribute has no effect because the queue will be deleted as soon as client disconnects (or its connection is lost). Auto-deleted queues are deleted when the last consumer is canceled (or its channel is closed, or its connection is lost).

If there never was a consumer it won't be deleted.

Arguments

Arguments (optional; used by plugins and broker-specific features such as message TTL, queue length limit, etc)

Time-to-live

In this part, you can set timespan to a queue which will discard if it reaches its lifespan which is set.

Time will be in milliseconds.

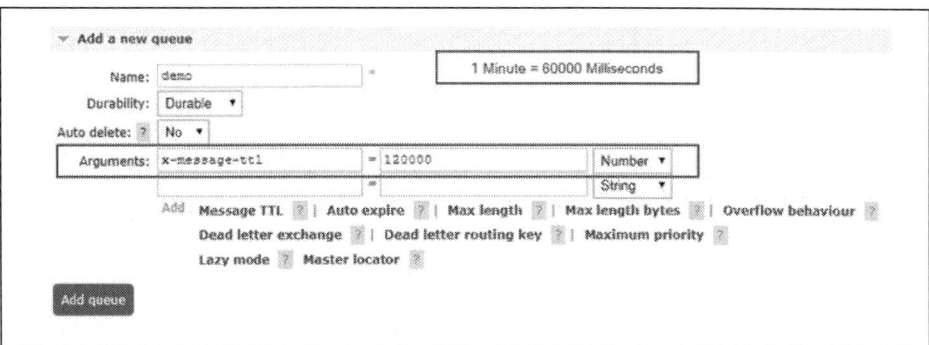

Auto expire

In this part, you can set expiry to a queue by setting this property.

This controls for how long a queue can be unused before it is automatically deleted.

Unused means the queue has no consumers, the queue has not been redeclared, and **basic.get** has not been invoked for a duration of at least the expiration period.

Max Length

How many (ready) messages a queue can contain before it starts to drop them from its head.

A maximum number of messages can be set by supplying the x-max-length queue declaration argument with a non-negative integer value.

For example, If you set value x-max-length = 2 and if you publish three messages in the queue then only two messages will be there, the oldest will be deleted from the queue.

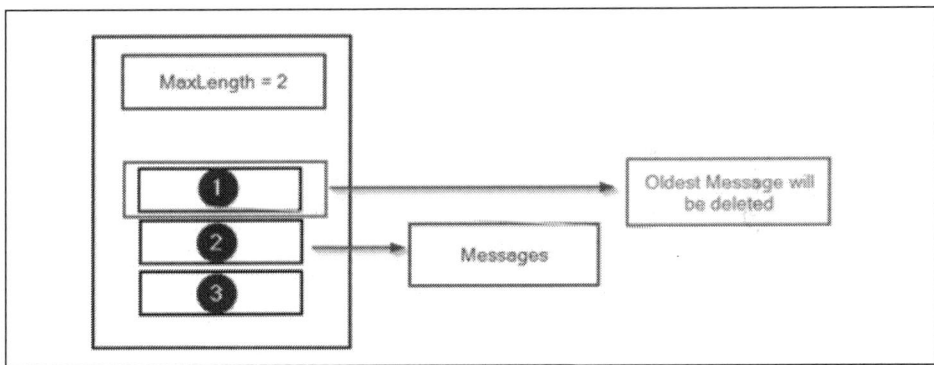

Max Length Bytes

Total body size for ready messages a queue can contain before it starts to drop them from its head.

Maximum length in bytes can be set by supplying the x-max-length-bytes queue declaration argument with a non-negative integer value.

(Sets the "x-max-length-bytes" argument.) *1000000 bytes = 1MB*

For example, If you set value *x-max-length-bytes = 1000000* and if you publish messages in queue and the queue size increase more than 1 MB then the oldest will be deleted from the queue (drop them from its head).

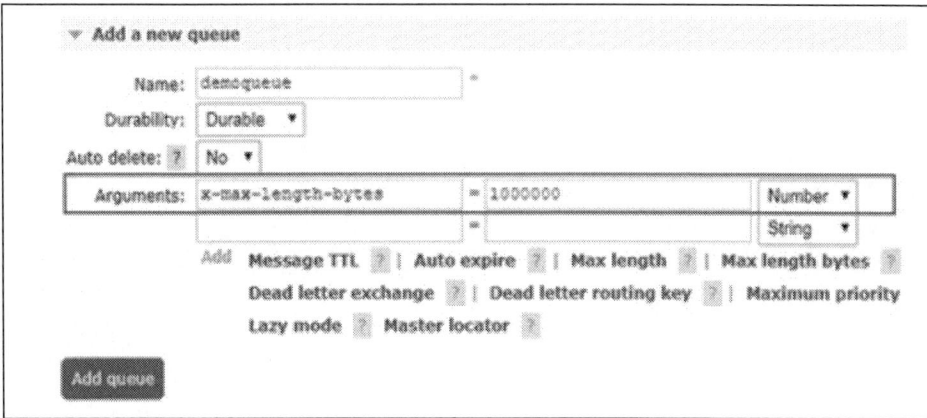

Overflow Behaviour

Sets the queue overflow behavior. This determines what happens to messages when the maximum length of a queue is reached. Valid values are drop-head or reject-publish.

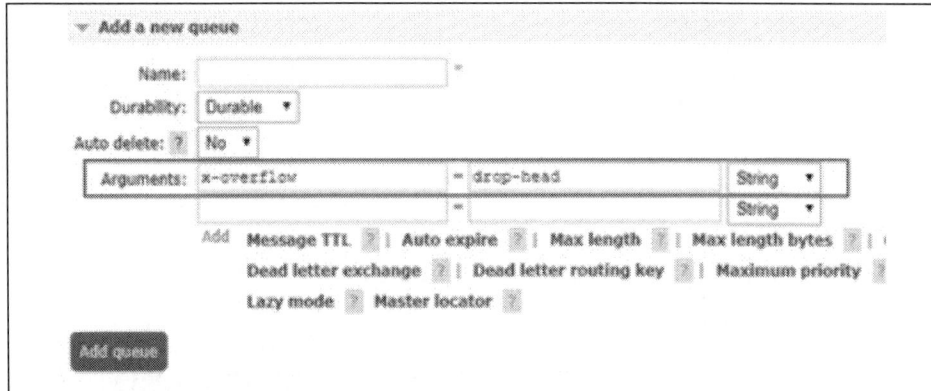

Dead Letter Exchange

Optional name of an exchange to which messages will be republished if they are rejected or expire.

Dead Letter Routing Key

Optional replacement routing key to use when a message is dead-lettered. If this is not set, the message's original routing key will be used.

For example, if you publish a message to an exchange with routing key foo, and that message is dead-lettered, it will be published to its dead letter exchange with routing key foo. If the queue the message originally landed on had been declared with x-dead-letter-routing-key set to bar, then the message will be published to its dead letter exchange with routing key bar.

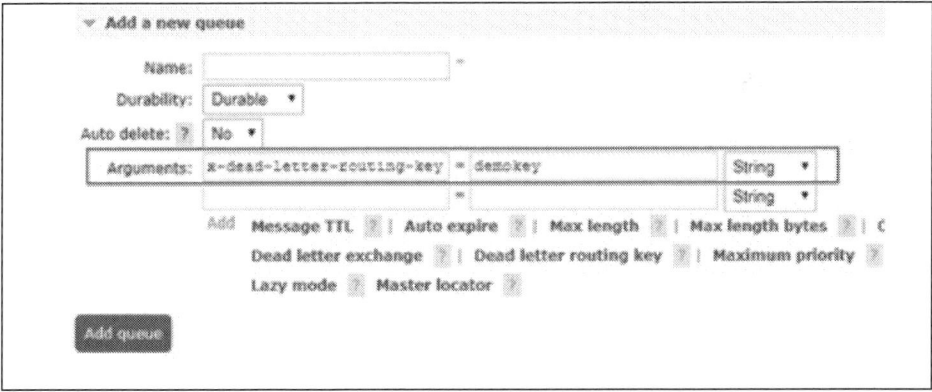

Maximum Priority

A maximum number of priority levels for the queue to support; if not set, the queue will not support message priorities.

(Sets the "x-max-priority" argument.)

To declare a priority queue, use the x-max-priority optional queue argument. This argument should be a positive integer between 1 and 255, indicating the maximum priority the queue should support.

![Add a new queue form with x-max-priority argument]

Lazy Mode

Set the queue into the lazy mode, keeping as many messages as possible on disk to reduce RAM usage; if not set, the queue will keep an in-memory cache to deliver messages as fast as possible.

(Sets the *x-queue-mode* argument.)

![Add a new queue form with x-queue-mode lazy argument]

Master Locator

Set the queue into master location mode, determining the rule by which the queue master is located when declared on a cluster of nodes.

(Sets the *x-queue-master-locator* argument.)

Adding Queue

To create a queue, you need to click on the queue tab in web management plugin.

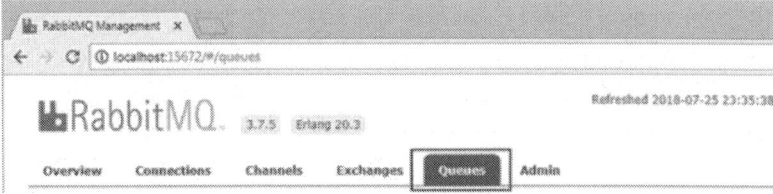

Learning RabbitMQ With C# 21

After clicking on queues tab, you will see add Queue panel with an arrow just click on that panel to expand.

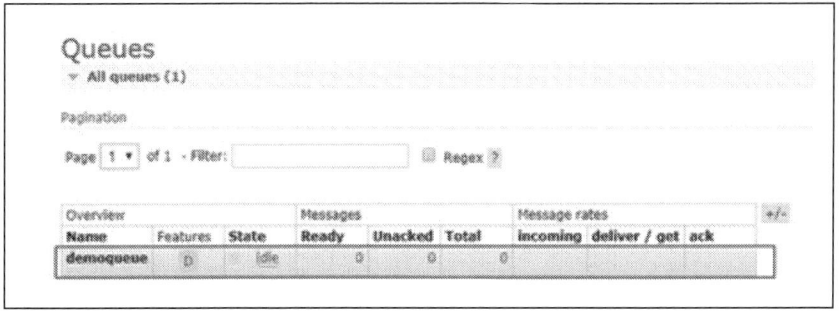

After clicking on Add a new panel queue will expand in that we are going enter queue details.

First, we are going to start with the name of the queue we are going to name it as **"demoqueue"** then we are going to choose durability as a Durable and final option, we are going set auto delete to No and click on Add queue button to create a queue.

After adding a queue, you can view queue which you have recently added, it is located just above add queue panel.

Binding in RabbitMQ

What is Binding

A binding is a connection which we can configure between a queue and an exchange.

Simple words: A binding is a relationship between an exchange and a queue.

In this part, we are going to bind exchange with queue using routing key and this will be used for direct type exchange. The exchange will route the request to particular queue on basis of routing key.

For binding, click on queue name which you have entered "**demoqueue**", after that click on it, bindings panel will expand, next it will ask for exchange name, enter exchange name which we have created "**demoexchange**" and routing key "**demokey**" and click on bind button.

Snapshot after binding

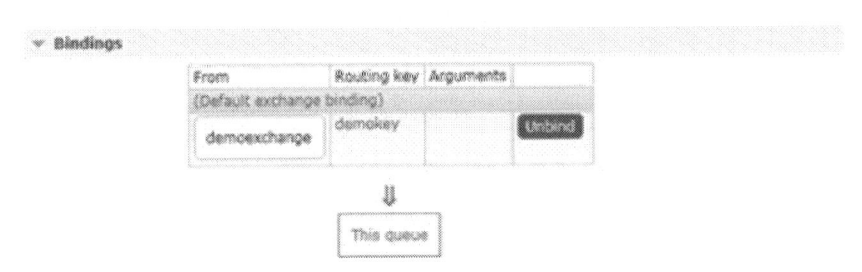

After binding if you want to unbind it then you can click on **Unbind** button to remove binding.

RabbitMQ Users

In this part, we are going to learn how to create a new User and give permission to New User.

For creating a New user, we need to login into Web Management Plugin using default credentials.

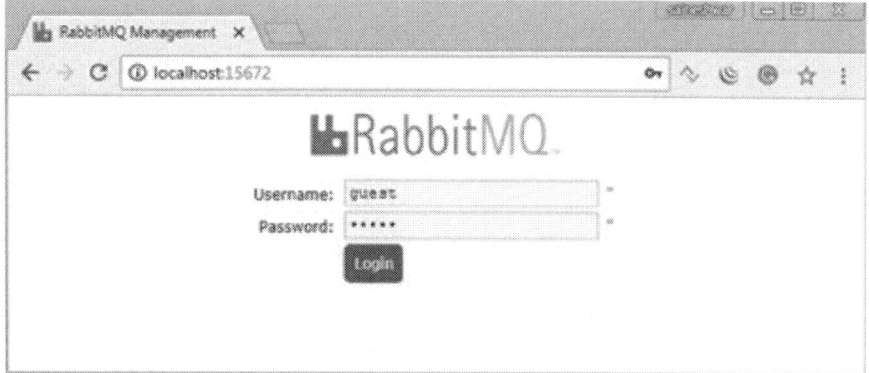

After logging into the application, we are going to choose **Admin** tab.

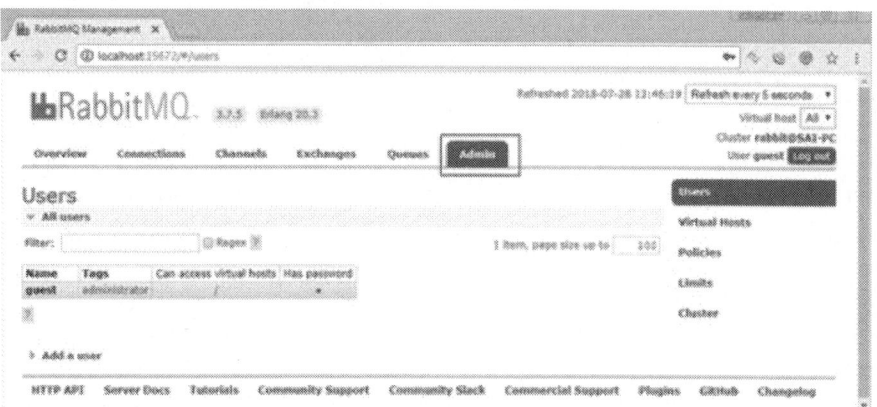

After choosing admin tab we can see a default username which is "guest" which has "administrator" (Tags) privilege below that we can see add new user panel.

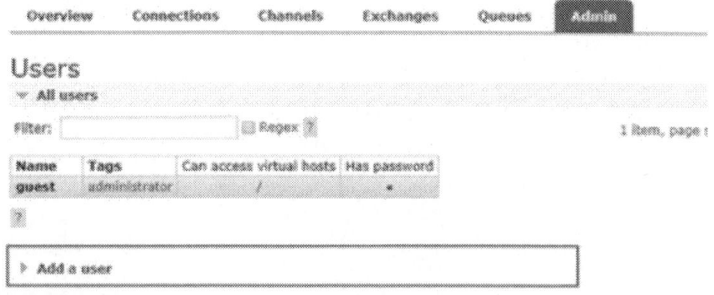

Clicking on **Add a User** panel to create new Users.

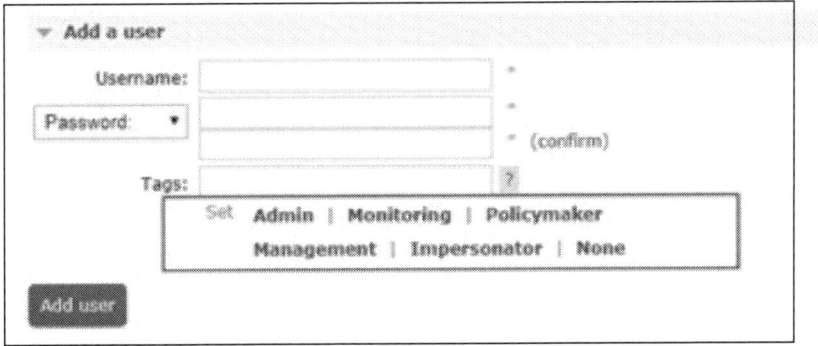

Before moving ahead lets first have a look at tags. Tags in this part are as rights (privileges) which are assigned to users which are created. We can set single or multiple privileges to a user if we want multiple privileges then just set privileges as comma-separated (administrator, management)

Currently Supported by the Management Plugin

Management

The user can access the management plugin.

Policymaker

The user can access the management plugin and manage policies and parameters for the vhosts they have access to.

Monitoring

The user can access the management plugin and see all connections and channels as well as node-related information.

Administrator

The user can do everything monitoring can do, manage users, vhosts, and permissions, close other user's connections, and manage policies and parameters for all vhosts.

Creating Users

In this part we are going to create new user and we are going to set Username as "**demouser**" after that we are going to set password as **123456** after that we are going set privilege to this user as "**administrator**" (just click on Admin link it will set "**administrator**" in tags field) finally click on **Add user** to create new user.

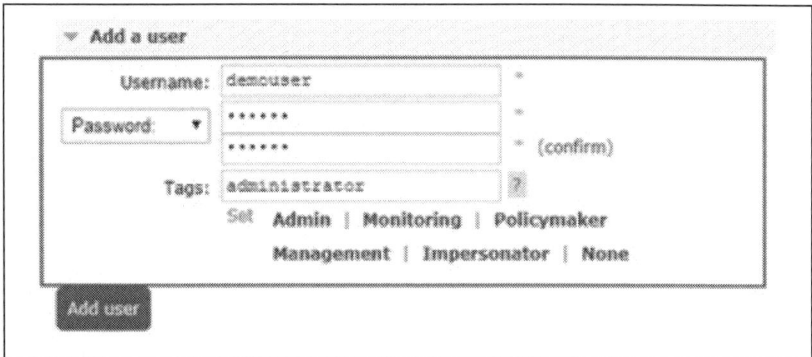

After adding a user, you can see all users in all user's panel just expand it. After expanding you can see the new user **demouser** but in the grid, you can see *can access virtual hosts* columns where it has the value **No access** which means we do not have the privilege to virtual hosts.

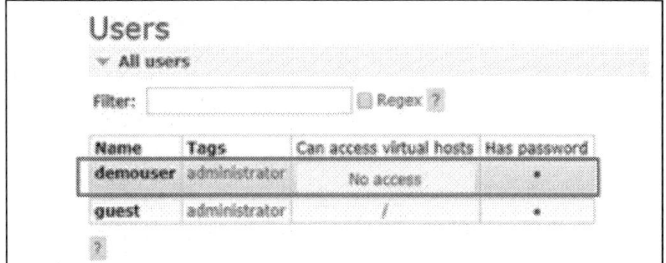

Setting Privilege to Access Virtual Hosts

For setting permission just click on username which we have created **demouser**.

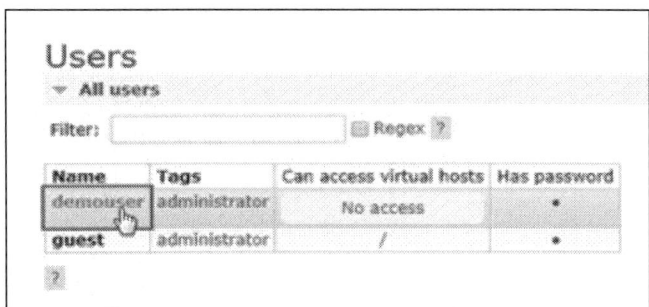

After clicking on **demouser** go to permission panel which is just below overview panel.

Just expand permission panel and click on set permission button to set permission to demouser.

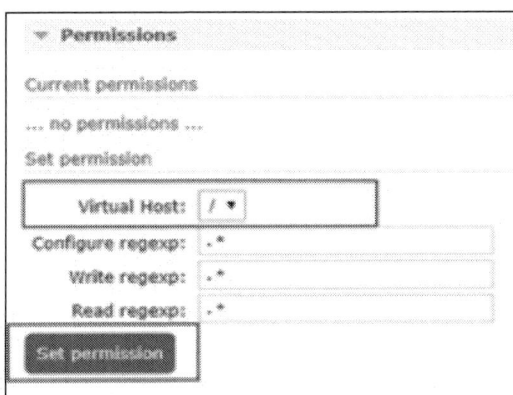

Once the permission is set, you'll see the **Current permissions** as shown below. Now you should be able to log in as this **demouser** to the RabbitMQ Web Management Plugin.

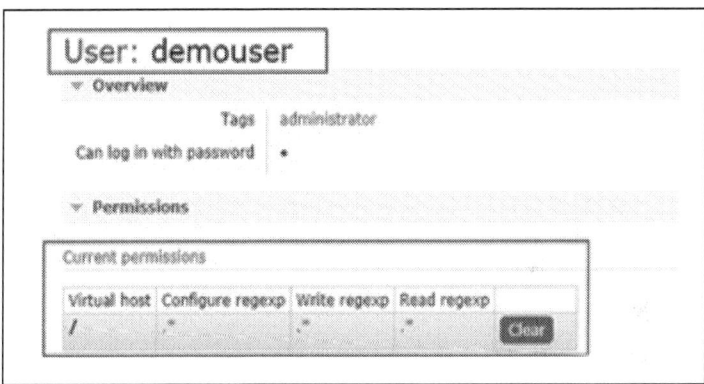

Let's login into RabbitMQ Web Management Plugin with new user **demouser**.

Following is the snapshot after logging into RabbitMQ Web Management Plugin with new user **demouser**.

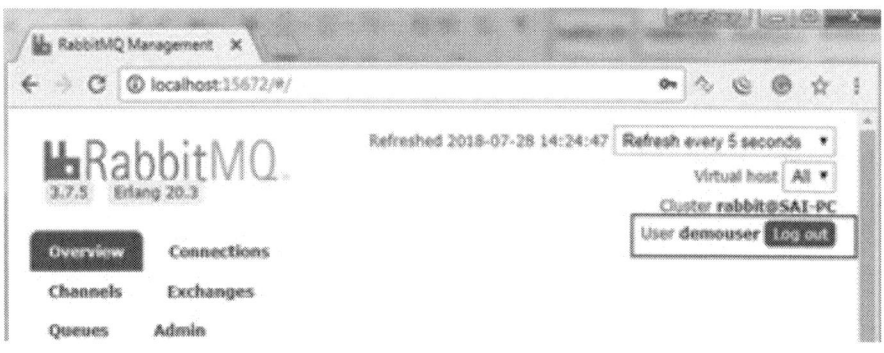

RabbitMQ Virtual Hosts

What are Virtual Hosts?

Virtual hosts are like a virtual box which contains a logical grouping of connections, exchanges, queues, bindings, user permissions, policies, and many more things.

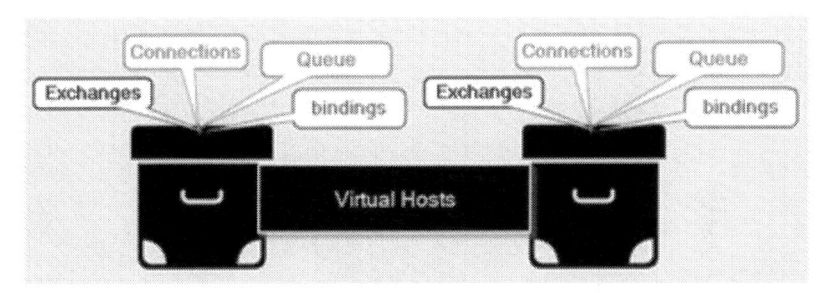

We can create different virtual host and each virtual host will have users.

Creating Virtual host

To create a new virtual host, we are first going to log in with default credentials and then we are going to choose admin tab.

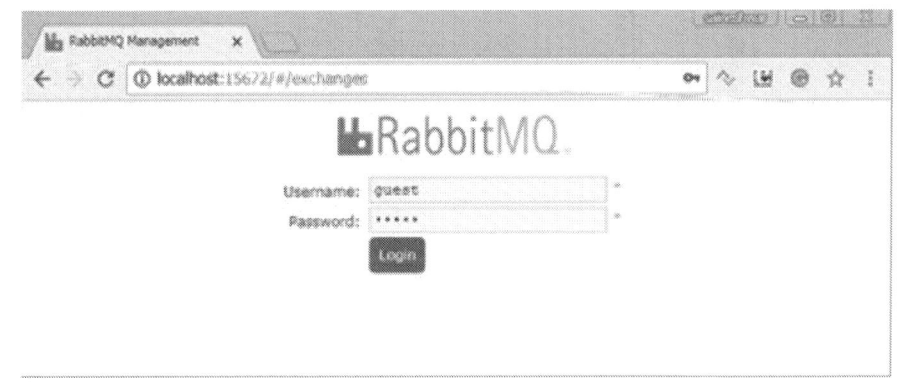

After choosing admin tab you will see vertical menus in right part of the page in that choose **Virtual Hosts**.

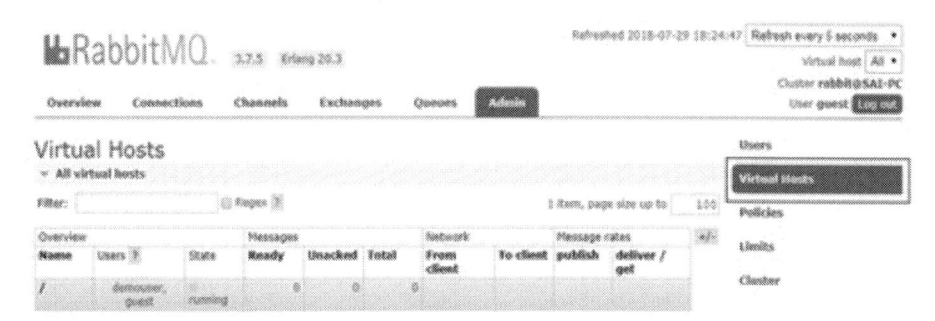

After choosing **Virtual Hosts** you will see the default **Virtual Hosts** which is already present below that there is a panel **Add a new virtual host** just click on it to expand.

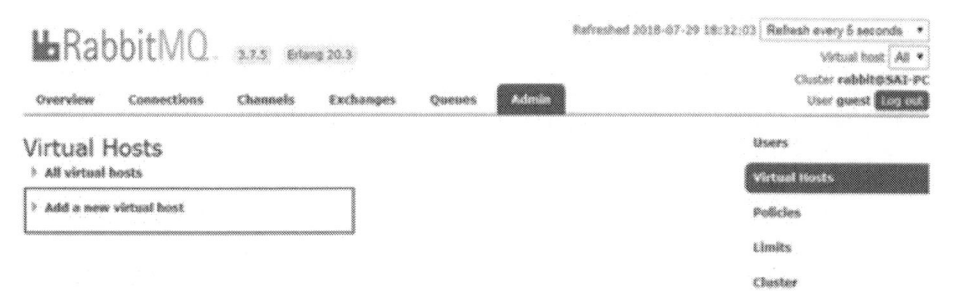

After expanding we can see for adding virtual host we need to add Name parameter here, I am entering the name as **demohost** next click on **Add a new virtual host** button to create **demohost** virtual host.

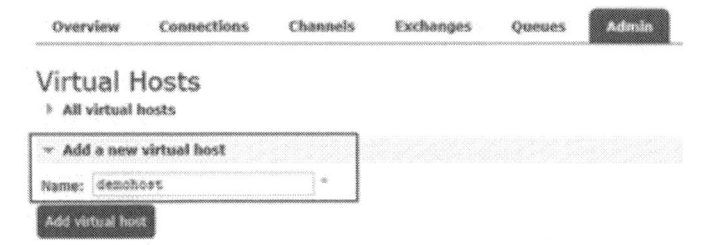

After adding a virtual host, we can see the newly added virtual host in **All virtual hosts** panel.

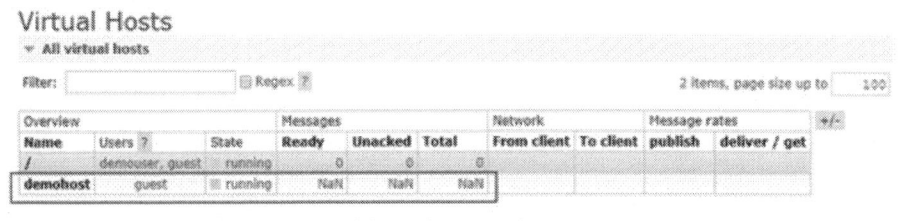

Till now, we have created virtual host but we have not assigned any user to this virtual host, let's create new User.

Creating Users

In this part we are going to create new user and we are going to set Username as **virtualuser** after that we are going to set password as *123456,* after that we are going set privilege to this user as **administrator** (just click on Admin link it will set **administrator** in tags field) finally click on **Add user** to create new user.

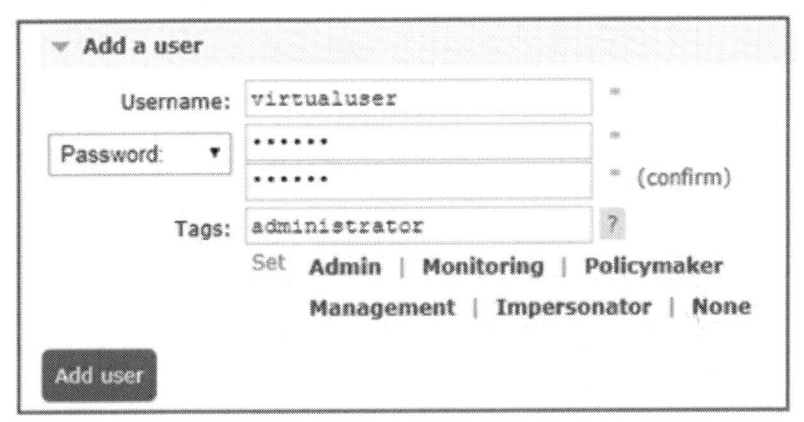

After adding a user, you can see all users in all user's panel just expand it. After expanding you can see the new user **virtualuser** but in the grid, you can see **Can access virtual hosts** columns where it has the value **No access** which means we do not have the privilege to virtual hosts.

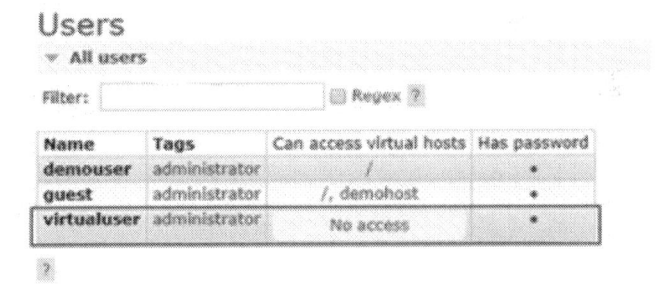

Setting Privilege to Access Virtual Hosts

For setting permission just click on username which we have created **virtualuser**.

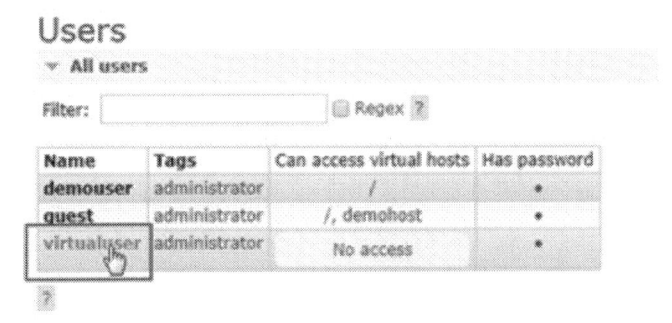

After clicking on **virtualuser** go to permission panel which is just below overview panel.

Just expand permission panel and just click on set permission button to set permission to **virtualuser**.

The default value is ".*" which allows access to all exchanges and queues in the virtual host.

Once the permission is set, you'll see the **Current permission** as shown follows:

Now you should be able to log in as this **virtualuser** to the RabbitMQ Web Management Plugin.

Let's login into RabbitMQ Web Management Plugin with new user **virtualuser**.

Following is the snapshot after logging into RabbitMQ Web Management Plugin with new user **virtualuser**.

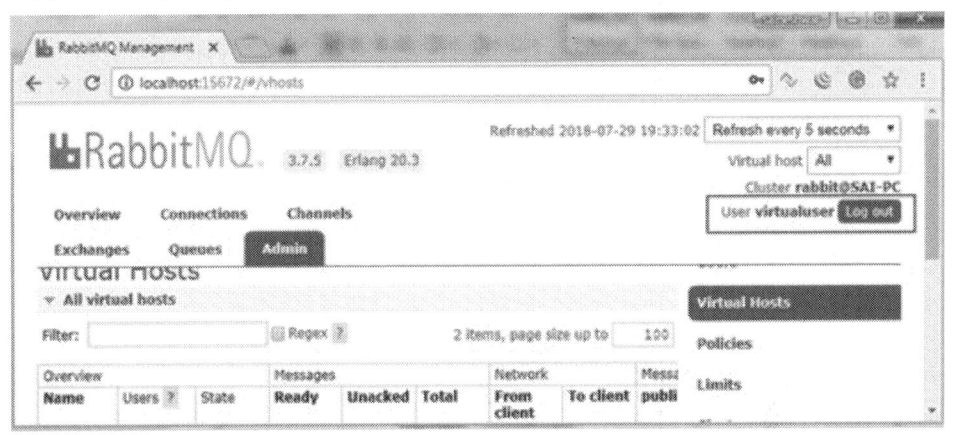

Now we have completed creating new virtual host along with that we have to assign a new user to it.

Connections

A connection is a TCP connection between your application and the RabbitMQ broker.

Referenced from: https://www.cloudamqp.com/blog/2015-05-18-part1-rabbitmq-for-beginners-what-is-rabbitmq.html

In connection tab it will show live connections of both producer of message and consumer of the message along with that it will show usernames of each connection with the state of connection if you are using SSL/TLS then it will indicate in the connection it will mark with a dark dot "." It will also show which protocol is been used after that in the network it will show from the client and to client network utilization.

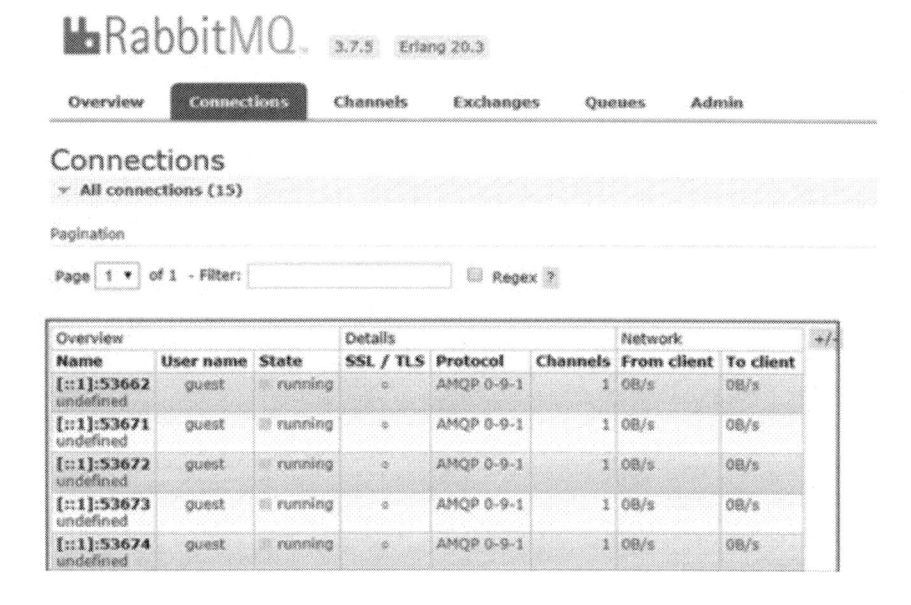

If you want to see details of each connection, then click on connection name.

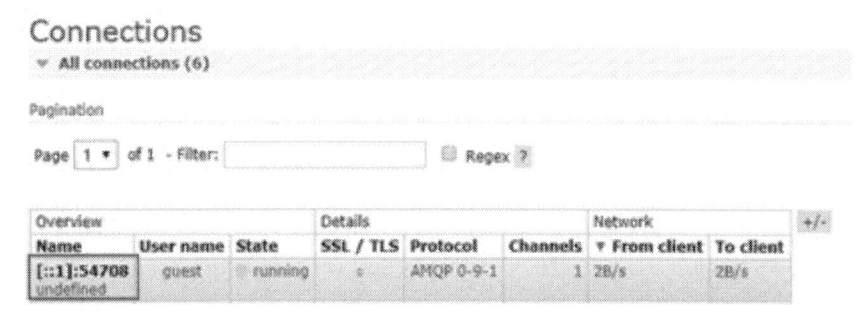

After clicking on connection name, it will show all details of connection along with data rates, channels, client properties, runtime metric, and finally close connection.

If you want to close connection, then you can open **Close this connection** tab type reason and click on **Force Close** button.

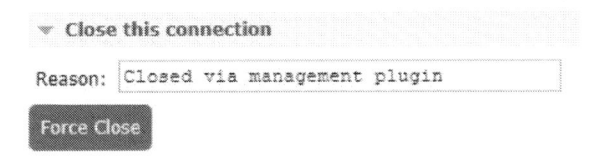

Channels

A channel is a virtual connection inside a connection. When you are publishing or consuming messages from a queue - it's all done over a channel.

Referenced from: https://www.cloudamqp.com/blog/2015-05-18-part1-rabbitmq-for-beginners-what-is-rabbitmq.html

In channel tab it will show live channels of both producer of message and consumer of the message along with that it will show mode. There are two modes. C – confirm channel will send streaming publish confirmations. T – transactional channel is transactional after that it will show state of channel. Next details in that we have Unconfirmed column it will show Number of published messages not yet confirmed next to Unconfirmed column is Prefetch column which shows details of per channel limit. Next to Prefetch column is Unacked column the Unacked means that the consumer has promised to process them but has not acknowledged that they are processed further we have message rates which show published and confirmed rates along with delivered and acknowledge details.

Note for Mode

Channel guarantee mode. Can be one of the following, or neither:

C – confirm

Channel will send streaming publish confirmations.

T – transactional

Channel is transactional.

Note for Prefetch count

Channel prefetch counts.

Each channel can have two prefetch counts: A per-consumer count, which will limit each new consumer created on the channel, and a global count, which is shared between all consumers on the channel.

This column shows one, the other, or both limits if they are set.

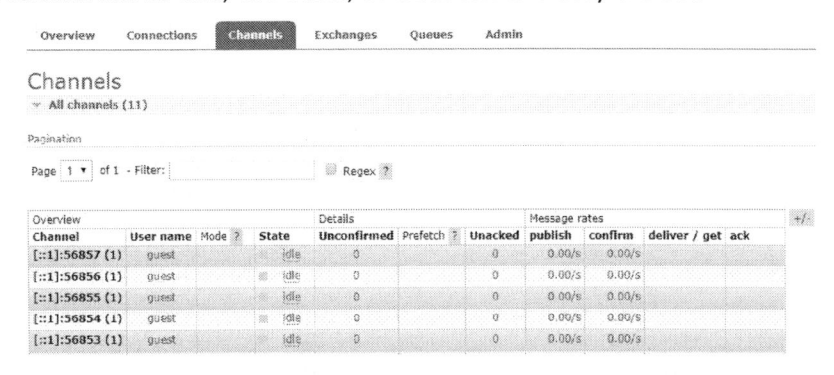

Overview			Details			Message rates			+/-
Channel	User name	Mode ?	State	Unconfirmed	Prefetch ?	Unacked	publish	confirm	deliver / get ack
[::1]:56857 (1)	guest		idle	0		0	0.00/s	0.00/s	
[::1]:56856 (1)	guest		idle	0		0	0.00/s	0.00/s	
[::1]:56855 (1)	guest		idle	0		0	0.00/s	0.00/s	
[::1]:56854 (1)	guest		idle	0		0	0.00/s	0.00/s	
[::1]:56853 (1)	guest		idle	0		0	0.00/s	0.00/s	

Learning RabbitMQ With C#

If you want to see details of each channel then click on **Channel** name **[::1]:57086 (1)** it will show all details related to that channel.

Publishing Message

For publishing a message, Login into web management plugin with credentials.

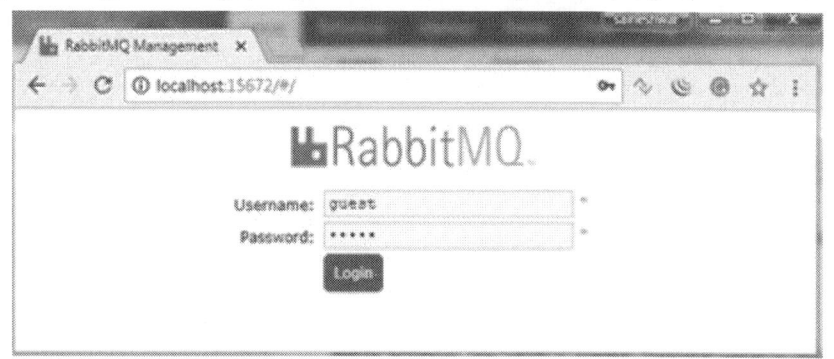

After logging into web management plugin next click on the queue (**demoqueue**).

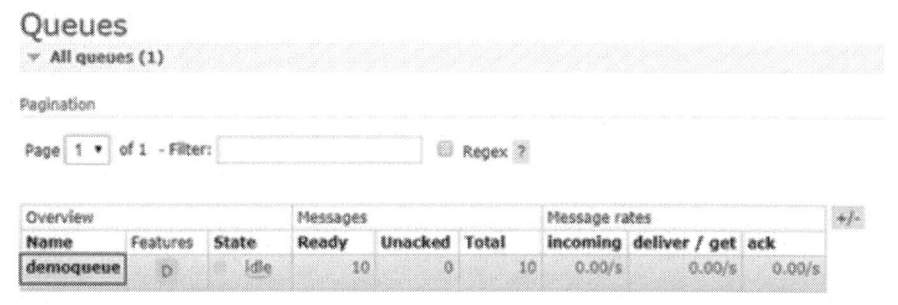

After clicking on demoqueue "queue" just below bindings panel is publish message panel in that just enter a message in Payload text area and click on publish message.

Snapshot after Publishing Message

Reading Message

For reading a message, Login into web management plugin with credentials.

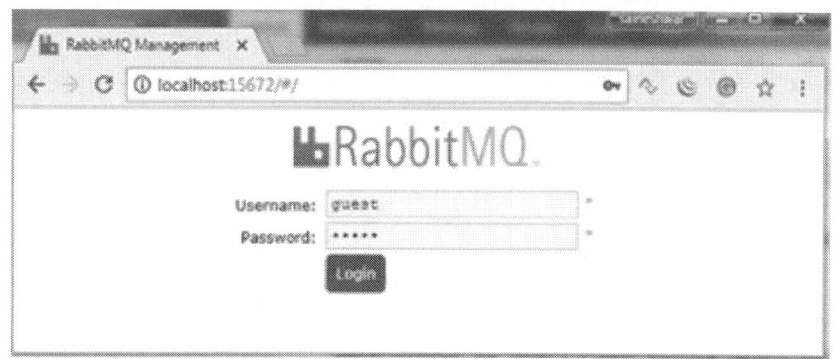

After logging into web management plugin, click on the queue (**demoqueue**).

Below published message is Get message, here you can read a message from **demoqueue** here in message textbox you can enter the count of messages to read from the queue and click on Get Message but to get Message.

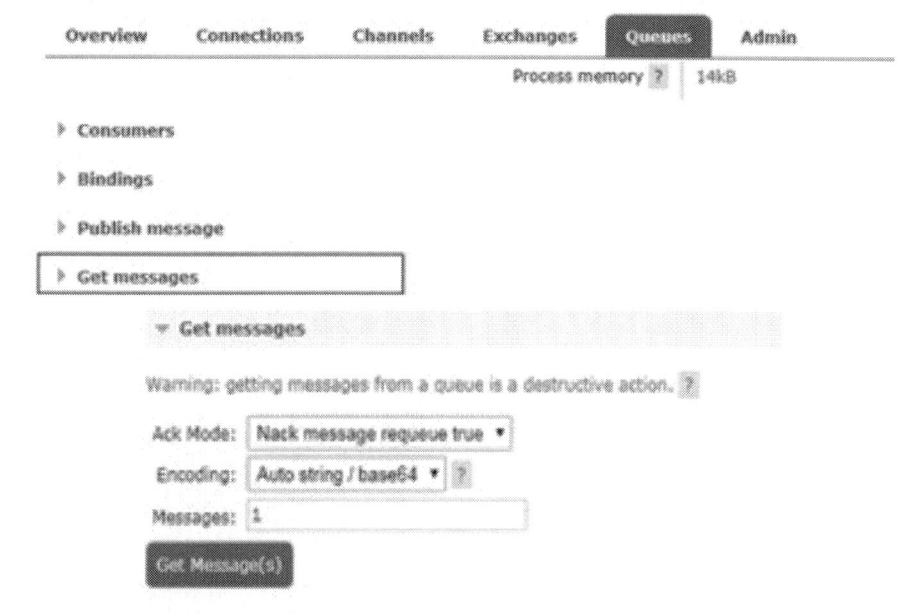

Learning RabbitMQ With C#

Snapshot while Reading the Message

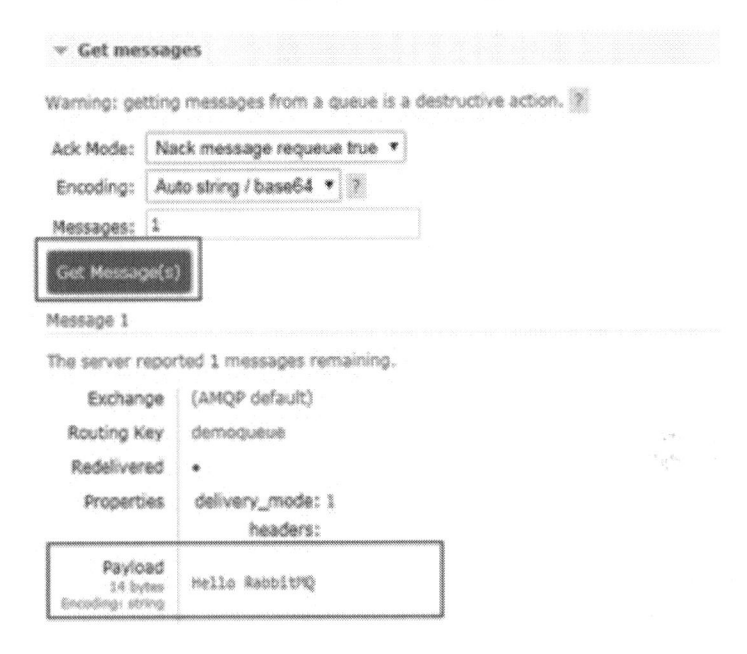

```
▼ Get messages

Warning: getting messages from a queue is a destructive action. ?
     Ack Mode:  Nack message requeue true  ▼
     Encoding:  Auto string / base64  ▼  ?
     Messages:  1

    [ Get Message(s) ]

Message 1
The server reported 1 messages remaining.
        Exchange  (AMQP default)
     Routing Key  demoqueue
      Redelivered  ●
       Properties  delivery_mode: 1
                   headers:
        ┌─────────────────────────────┐
        │   Payload                   │
        │     14 bytes   Hello RabbitMQ│
        │   Encoding: string          │
        └─────────────────────────────┘
```

After reading the message, the last part we are going to see is Deleting Queue.

Delete Message

For deleting a message, Login into web management plugin with credentials.

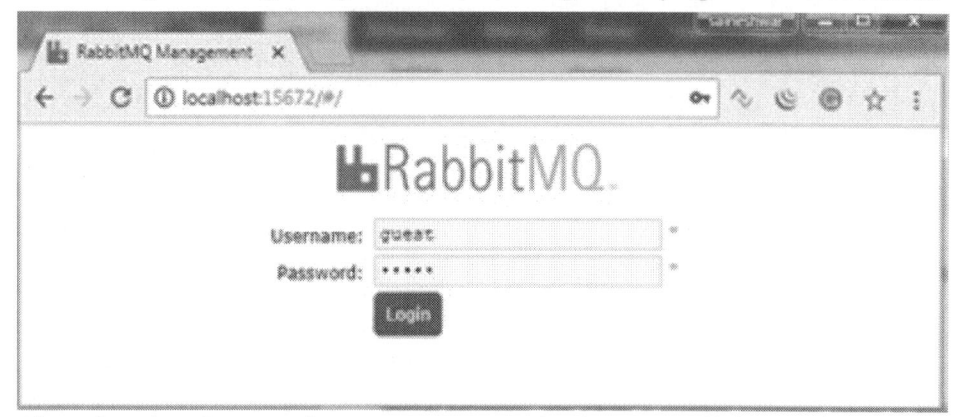

After logging into web management plugin next click on the queue (**demoqueue**).

To delete the message, you can expand delete panel in that you will see only delete button. Just click on it to delete.

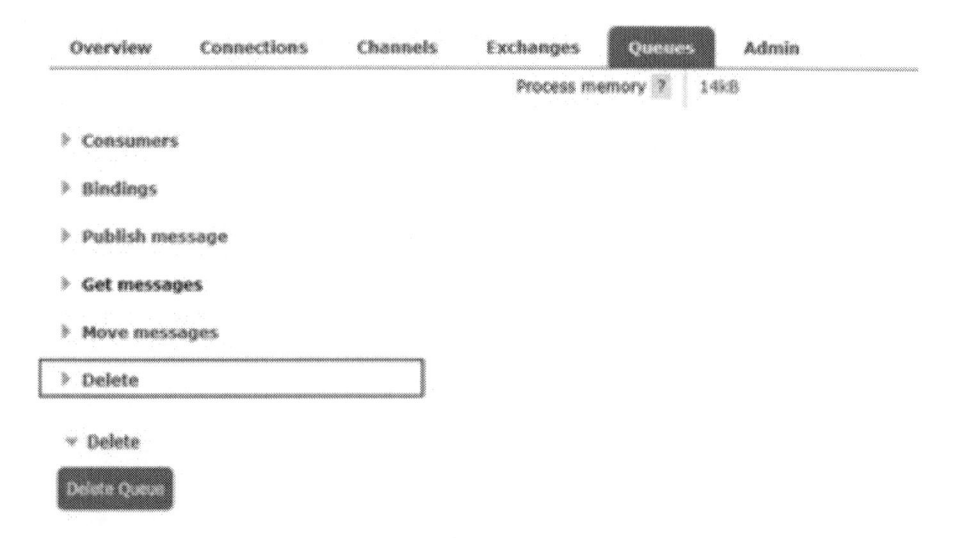

After clicking on **Delete Queue** button, a message will pop up it will ask for confirmation as shown above below:

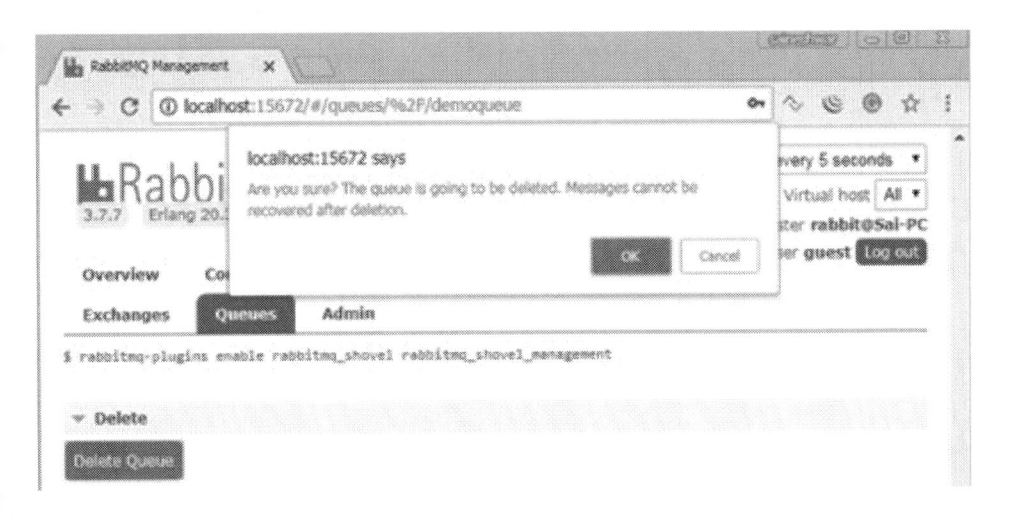

If we click on the **OK** button it will delete the queue.

Publish Message Using C# to RabbitMQ

In this part, we are going to learn how to Publish a Message to RabbitMQ using .Net Application and RabbitMQ.Client in step by step way.

Creating RequestRabbitMQ Application

Let's create a simple console application with Name **RequestRabbitMQ**.

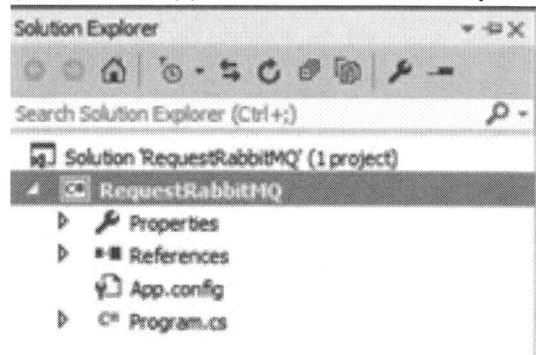

After creating application, we are going to add **RabbitMQ.Client** NuGet package.

Adding RabbitMQ.Client NuGet Package

In this part for creating a connection with the RabbitMQ server to create request, we need to add **RabbitMQ.Client** package from NuGet Package.

Command to install: Install-Package **RabbitMQ.Client -Version 5.1.0**

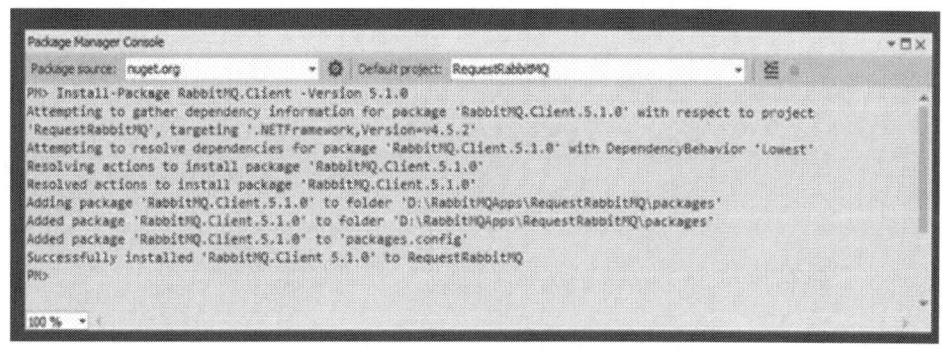

After installing NuGet package of **RabbitMQ.Client** next we are going to create an exchange from web admin console.

Adding Direct Exchange

In this part, we are going to create an exchange for doing that we have first created a connection to RabbitMQ server using RabbitMQ.Client after creating connection next we have passed credentials along with HostName to connectionFactory after that we have created a connection by calling **CreateConnection** method, next to add exchange we have called method **ExchangeDeclare** method and passed parameters such as *exchange name* and *exchange type*.

Code Snippet

```csharp
using RabbitMQ.Client;
using System;

namespace RequestRabbitMQ
{
    class Program
    {
        static void Main(string[] args)
        {
            string UserName = "guest";
            string Password = "guest";
            string HostName = "localhost";

            //Main entry point to the RabbitMQ .NET AMQP client
            var connectionFactory = new RabbitMQ.Client.ConnectionFactory()
            {
                UserName = UserName,
                Password = Password,
                HostName = HostName
            };

            var connection = connectionFactory.CreateConnection();
            var model = connection.CreateModel();

            //// Create Exchange
            model.ExchangeDeclare("demoExchange", ExchangeType.Direct);

            Console.ReadLine();
        }
    }
}
```

Let's check result by running application.

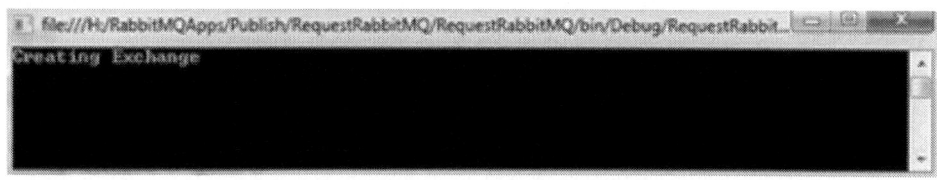

After adding exchange let's check web management plugin you will see we have successfully created exchanges.

Overview	Connections	Channels	Exchanges	Queues	Admin
amq.direct	direct	D			
amq.fanout	fanout	D			
amq.headers	headers	D			
amq.match	headers	D			
amq.rabbitmq.trace	topic	D I			
amq.topic	topic	D			
demoExchange	direct				

Adding Queue

Now we are going to add a queue.

For doing that we are going to add call **QueueDeclare** method and pass parameters to it.

Method definition:

```
//
// Summary:
//     Declare a queue.
[AmqpMethodDoNotImplement(null)]
QueueDeclareOk QueueDeclare(string queue, bool durable, bool exclusive, bool autoDelete, IDictionary<string, object> arguments);
//
```

First parameter is queue name **demoqueue**.

The second parameter is Durable **true**.

The third parameter is Exclusive **false**.

The fourth parameter is autodelete **false**.

Fifth parameter is Arguments **null**.

```
// Create Queue
model.QueueDeclare("demoqueue", true, false, false, null);
```

Code Snippet

```
using RabbitMQ.Client;
using System;
```

```csharp
namespace RequestRabbitMQ
{
    class Program
    {
        static void Main(string[] args)
        {
            string UserName = "guest";
            string Password = "guest";
            string HostName = "localhost";

            //Main entry point to the RabbitMQ .NET AMQP client
            var connectionFactory = new RabbitMQ.Client.ConnectionFactory()
            {
                UserName = UserName,
                Password = Password,
                HostName = HostName
            };

            var connection = connectionFactory.CreateConnection();
            var model = connection.CreateModel();

            //// Create Exchange
            //model.ExchangeDeclare("demoExchange", ExchangeType.Direct);
            //Console.WriteLine("Creating Exchange");

            // Create Queue
            model.QueueDeclare("demoqueue", true, false, false, null);
            Console.WriteLine("Creating Queue");

            Console.ReadLine();
        }
    }
}
```

Let's check the result by running application.

After adding queue let's check web management plugin you will see we have successfully created the queue.

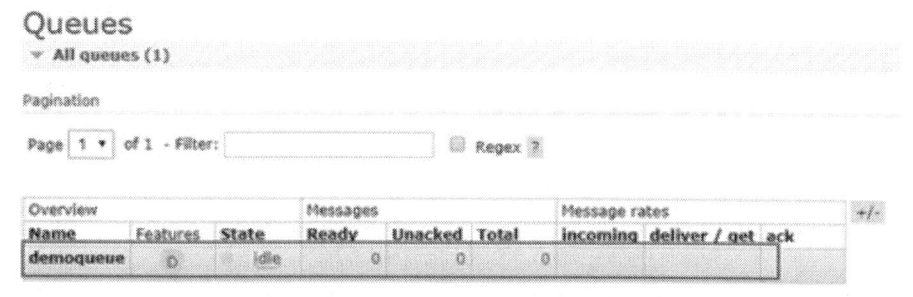

Queues

Overview			Messages			Message rates		
Name	Features	State	Ready	Unacked	Total	incoming	deliver / get	ack
demoqueue		idle	0	0	0			

After adding queue, we are going to bind queue with the exchange.

Binding the Demoqueue with demoExchange

In binding, we are going to enter the name of exchange **demoExchange** and we are going to enter routing key as **directexchange_key**.

Method definition:

```
//
// Summary:
//    /// (Spec method) Binds a queue. ///
public static void QueueBind(this IModel model, string queue, string exchange, string routingKey, IDictionary<string, object> arguments = null);
//
```

First parameter is queue name **demoqueue**.

The second parameter is Exchange **demoExchange**.

Third parameter is routing key **directexchange_key**.

```
// Creating Binding
model.QueueBind("demoqueue",    "demoExchange",
"directexchange_key");
Console.WriteLine("Creating Binding");
```

Code Snippet

```
using RabbitMQ.Client;
using System;

namespace RequestRabbitMQ
{
    class Program
    {
        static void Main(string[] args)
        {
            string UserName = "guest";
            string Password = "guest";
            string HostName = "localhost";
```

```csharp
            //Main entry point to the RabbitMQ .NET AMQP client
            var connectionFactory = new RabbitMQ.Client.ConnectionFactory()
            {
                UserName = UserName,
                Password = Password,
                HostName = HostName
            };

            var connection = connectionFactory.CreateConnection();
            var model = connection.CreateModel();

            //// Create Exchange
                //model.ExchangeDeclare("demoExchange", ExchangeType.Direct);
                //Console.WriteLine("Creating Exchange");

            //// Create Queue
                //model.QueueDeclare("demoqueue", true, false, false, null);
                //Console.WriteLine("Creating Queue");

            // Creating Binding
               model.QueueBind("demoqueue", "demoExchange", "directexchange_key");
               Console.WriteLine("Creating Binding");

               Console.ReadLine();
        }
    }
}
```

After creating binding let's check web management plugin you will see we have successfully created the binding.

![Screenshot of RabbitMQ management UI showing Queues tab with Consumers and Bindings sections. Bindings table shows From: demoExchange, Routing key: directexchange_key, with an Unbind button. An arrow points down to "This queue".]

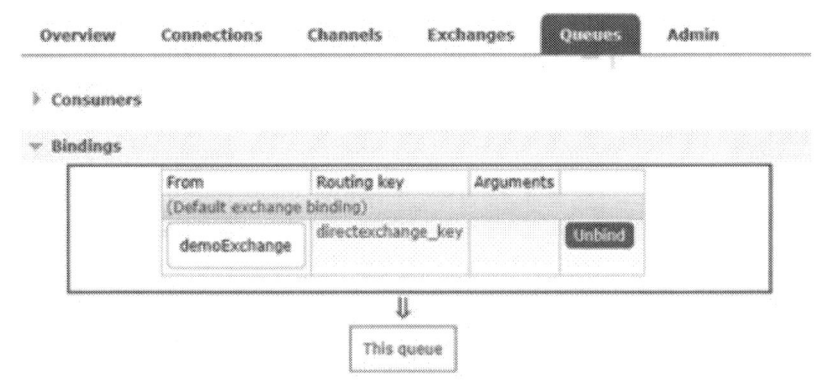

Now let's create push message to **demoqueue** from a console application.

Adding a Directmessages Class

We have created a **Directmessage** class, in this class we are going to create request and push to RabbitMQ.

First, we have declared Username, Password, and HostName as constant. After that, we have created a method with name **SendMessage** in that message we have created a connection to RabbitMQ server using RabbitMQ.Client after creating connection next we have passed credentials along with HostName to connectionFactory.

Next, we have written a simple message **Direct Message** and got it in bytes array form, finally, we are going to assign all these values to a BasicPublish method of **RabbitMQ.Client**.

Method definition

```
/// <summary>
/// (Extension method) Convenience overload of BasicPublish.
/// </summary>
/// <remarks>The publication occurs with mandatory=false</remarks>
public static void BasicPublish(this IModel model, string exchange, string routingKey, IBasicProperties basicProperties, byte[] body)
{
    model.BasicPublish(exchange, routingKey, false, basicProperties, body);
}
```

The parameter passed to it

Exchange: demoExchange

Routing key: directexchange_key

Code Snippet

```
using RabbitMQ.Client;
using System;
using System.Text;

namespace RequestRabbitMQ
{
    class Program
    {
        {
```

```csharp
static void Main(string[] args)
{
    string UserName = "guest";
    string Password = "guest";
    string HostName = "localhost";

    //Main entry point to the RabbitMQ .NET AMQP client
    var connectionFactory = new RabbitMQ.Client.ConnectionFactory()
    {
        UserName = UserName,
        Password = Password,
        HostName = HostName
    };

    var connection = connectionFactory.CreateConnection();
    var model = connection.CreateModel();

    //// Create Exchange
    //model.ExchangeDeclare("demoExchange", ExchangeType.Direct);
    //Console.WriteLine("Creating Exchange");

    //// Create Queue
    //model.QueueDeclare("demoqueue", true, false, false, null);
    //Console.WriteLine("Creating Queue");

    // Creating Binding
    //model.QueueBind("demoqueue", "demoExchange", "directexchange_key");
    //Console.WriteLine("Creating Binding");

    var properties = model.CreateBasicProperties();
    properties.Persistent = false;

    byte[] messagebuffer = Encoding.Default.GetBytes("Direct Message");

    model.BasicPublish("demoExchange", "directexchange_key", properties, messagebuffer);
    Console.WriteLine("Message Sent");
```

```
            Console.ReadLine();
        }
    }
}
```

After completing entire process let's save the application and run, after running the application you will see a message on console window as "message sent" just for notification.

After sending a message now let's have a look on the queue (demoqueue).

Now Let's See queue status "demoqueue"

If you see Queues status you will see **Ready "1"** which means we have successfully published a message to **demoqueue**.

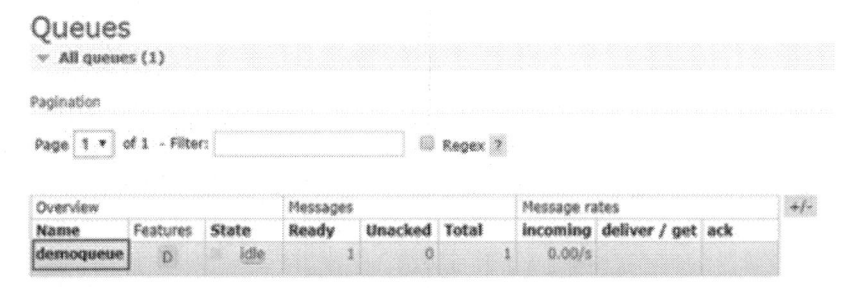

Consume Message Using C# to RabbitMQ

In this part we are going to learn how to consume messages from RabbitMQ using .Net in step by step way.

Creating RabbitMQConsumer Application

Let's create another console application for consuming messages from a queue with the name **RabbitMQConsumer**.

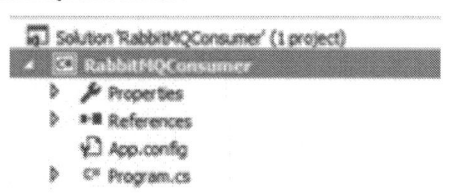

After creating application next we are going to add **RabbitMQ.Client** NuGet package.

Adding RabbitMQ.Client NuGet Package

In this part for creating a connection with RabbitMQ server to c. we need to add **RabbitMQ.Client** package from NuGet Package.
Command to install: Install-Package **RabbitMQ.Client -Version 5.1.0**

After installing *RabbitMQ.Client* next we are going to add a class with name **MessageReceiver**.

Code snippet of MessageReceiver class

In this part, we have created *MessageReceiver* class and this class inherits *DefaultBasicConsumer* class which is from RabbitMQ.Client next we have to override *HandleBasicDeliver* method this method receives message body next, we are going to write these messages as we can see in its console.

```
using System;
using System.Text;
using RabbitMQ.Client;

namespace RabbitMQConsumer
{
    public class MessageReceiver : DefaultBasicConsumer
    {
        private readonly IModel _channel;

        public MessageReceiver(IModel channel)
        {
            _channel = channel;
        }

        public override void HandleBasicDeliver(string consumerTag, ulong deliveryTag, bool redelivered, string exchange, string routingKey, IBasicProperties properties, byte[] body)
        {
            Console.WriteLine($"Consuming Message");
```

```
                    Console.WriteLine(string.Concat("Message
received from the exchange ", exchange));
                Console.WriteLine(string.Concat("Consumer tag:
", consumerTag));
                Console.WriteLine(string.Concat("Delivery tag:
", deliveryTag));
              Console.WriteLine(string.Concat("Routing tag: ",
routingKey));
                Console.WriteLine(string.Concat("Message: ",
Encoding.UTF8.GetString(body)));
            _channel.BasicAck(deliveryTag, false);
        }
    }
}
```

After completing with understanding code snippet of MessageReceiver class next we are going to call this class in the main method.

Code snippet of Main Method

In the main method we have created *ConnectionFactory* class and passed credentials and Hostname after that we have created connection, next we have created channel and set *prefetchCount* to 1 such that it tells RabbitMQ not to give more than one message to a worker at a time, Next, we have created instance of *MessageReceiver* class and passed IModel (channel) to it, in final step we have called **BasicConsume** method and passed queue name to it **demoqueue** along with this we have set autoAck to false and passed the **messageReceiver** instance to it.

```
using System;
using System.Collections.Generic;
using System.Linq;
using System.Text;
using System.Threading.Tasks;
using RabbitMQ.Client;

namespace RabbitMQConsumer
{
    class Program
    {
        private const string UserName = "guest";
        private const string Password = "guest";
        private const string HostName = "localhost";

        static void Main(string[] args)
```

```csharp
        {
            ConnectionFactory connectionFactory = new ConnectionFactory
            {
                HostName = **HostName**,
                UserName = **UserName**,
                Password = **Password**,
            };

            var connection = connectionFactory.CreateConnection();
            var channel = connection.CreateModel();

            // accept only one unack-ed message at a time
            // uint prefetchSize, ushort prefetchCount, bool global

            channel.BasicQos(0, 1, false);

            MessageReceiver messageReceiver = new MessageReceiver(channel);
            channel.BasicConsume("demoqueue", false, messageReceiver);

            Console.ReadLine();
        }
    }
}
```

Note: prefetchCount

In order to defeat that we can set the prefetch count with the value of 1. This tells RabbitMQ not to give more than one message to a worker at a time. Or, in other words, don't dispatch a new message to a worker until it has processed and acknowledged the previous one. Instead, it will dispatch it to the next worker that is not still busy.

Now we have complete working mechanism. Let's create request from **RequestRabbitMQ** console and consume a message from **RabbitMQConsumer** application.

Queue is Empty

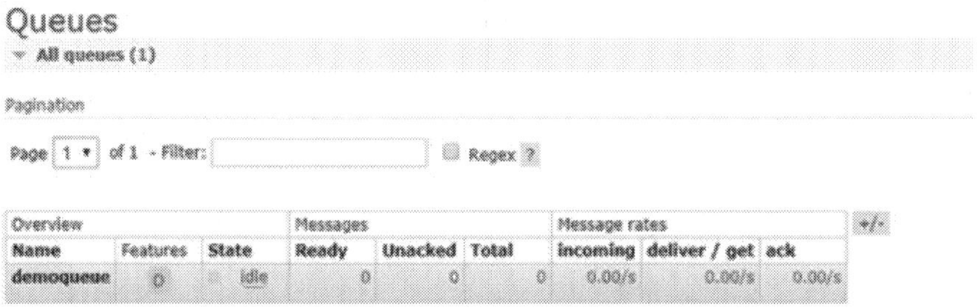

```
Queues
  All queues (1)
Pagination
  Page 1 ▼ of 1 - Filter:              Regex ?
```

Overview			Messages			Message rates			+/-
Name	Features	State	Ready	Unacked	Total	incoming	deliver / get	ack	
demoqueue	0	idle	0	0	0	0.00/s	0.00/s	0.00/s	

After we saw that queue (demoqueue) is empty, we are going to publish message to demoqueue.

Publishing Message

```
var connection = connectionFactory.CreateConnection();
var model = connection.CreateModel();

Create Exchange | Create Queue | Creating Binding

var properties = model.CreateBasicProperties();
properties.Persistent = false;

byte[] messagebuffer = Encoding.Default.GetBytes("Direct Message");

model.BasicPublish("demoExchange", "directexchange_key", properties, messagebuffer);
Console.WriteLine("Message Sent");

Console.ReadLine();
```

After we have published message now let's have a view on (queue) demoqueue.

Queue after Publishing Message

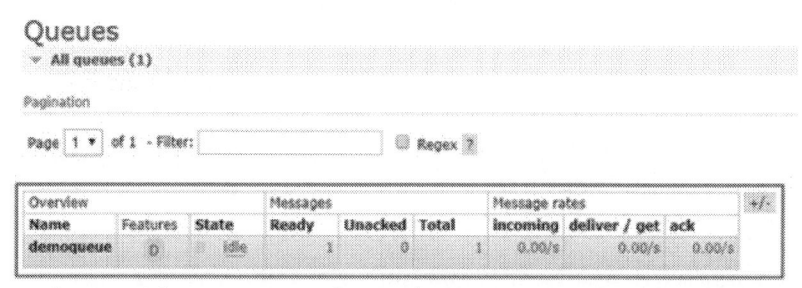

```
Queues
  All queues (1)
Pagination
  Page 1 ▼ of 1 - Filter:              Regex ?
```

Overview			Messages			Message rates			+/-
Name	Features	State	Ready	Unacked	Total	incoming	deliver / get	ack	
demoqueue	0	idle	1	0	1	0.00/s	0.00/s	0.00/s	

After we have push message to (queue) demoqueue the console application will start consuming it, following is the snapshot:

Consumed Message from demoqueue

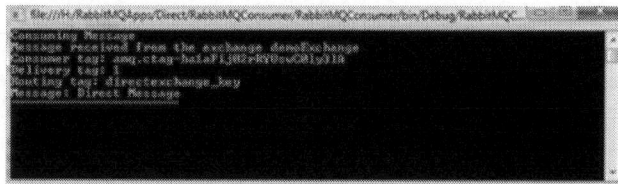

```
Consuming Message
Message received from the exchange demoExchange
Consumer tag: amq.ctag-halaFijU2rRYOcwCRlyOlh
Delivery tag: 1
Routing tag: directexchange_key
Message: Direct Message
```

Finally, we have completed consuming message from RabbitMQ queue.

Using RabbitMQ Direct Message Exchanges with .Net Application

In this part, we are going to use Direct Message Exchanges and push messages into RabbitMQ using .Net Application and RabbitMQ.Client and read messages from RabbitMQ using .Net Application and RabbitMQ.Client in step by step way.

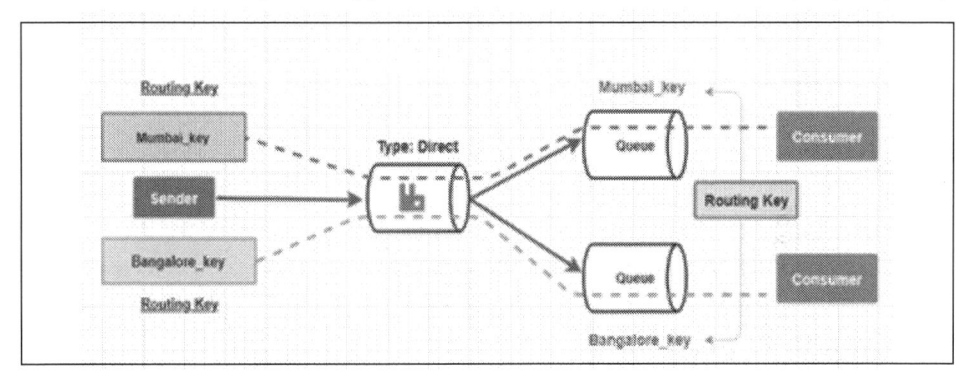

Types of Exchanges

1. Direct
2. fanout
3. Headers
4. Topic

Details of Exchanges

1. **Direct**: A direct exchange delivers messages to queues based on a message routing key.

   In a direct exchange, the message is routed to the queues whose binding key exactly matches the routing key of the message.
2. **Fanout**: A fanout exchange routes messages to all of the queues that are bound to it.
3. **Topic**: The topic exchange does a wildcard match between the routing key and the routing pattern specified in the binding.
4. **Headers**: Headers exchanges use the message header attributes for routing.

Creating RequestRabbitMQ Application

Let's Create a simple console application with the name **RequestRabbitMQ**.

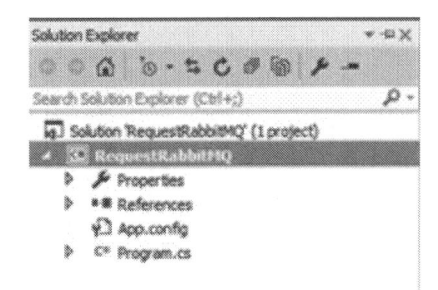

After creating application next we are going to add **RabbitMQ.Client** NuGet package.

Adding RabbitMQ.Client NuGet Package

In this part for creating a connection with RabbitMQ server to create request, we need to add **RabbitMQ.Client** package from NuGet Package.

Command to install: - Install-Package *RabbitMQ.Client -Version 5.1.0*

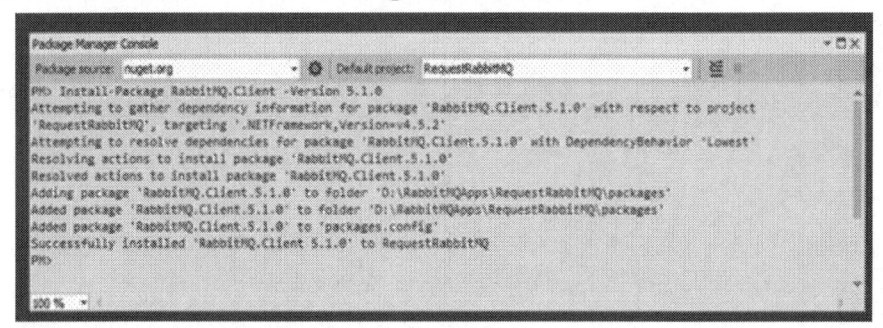

After installing NuGet package of **RabbitMQ.Client** next we are going to create an exchange from web admin console.

Adding Direct Exchange

Go to http://localhost:15672/#/exchanges, name exchange as request.exchange after entering name, we select Type as direct and click on Add exchange button to create.

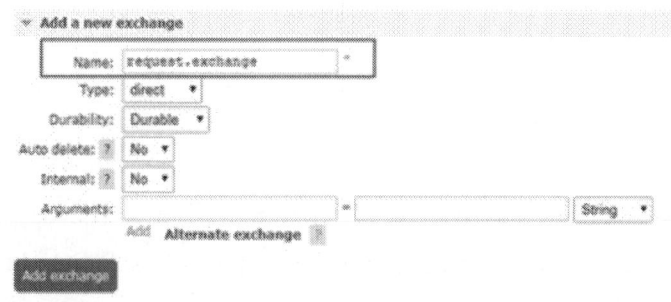

After adding exchange (**request.exchange**) next we are going to add Queue (request Queue).

Adding Queue

Go to http://localhost:15672/#/queues, add queue: request.queue.

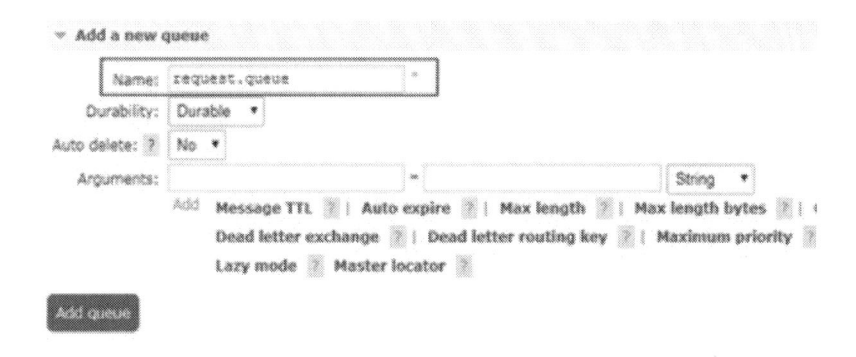

After adding queue next we are going to bind queue with exchange.

Binding the request.queue with request.exchange

In binding, we are going to enter the name of exchange **request.exchange** and we are going to enter routing key as **directexchange_key**.

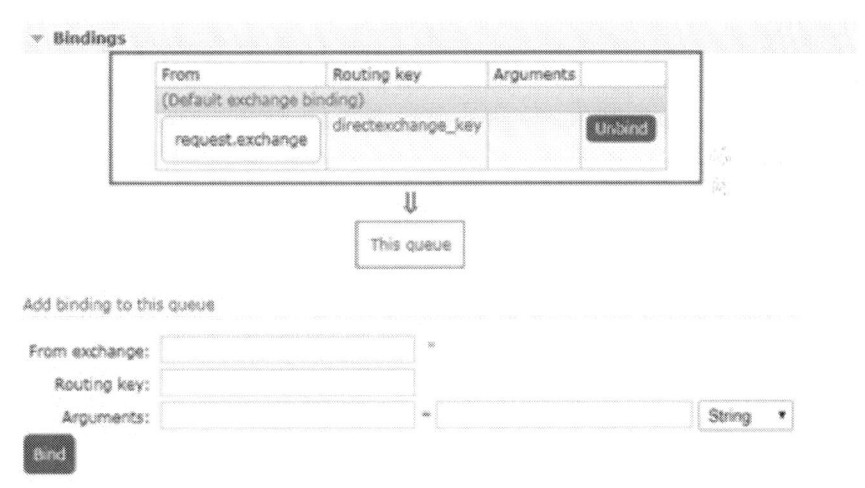

Now let's Create Push Message to **request.queue** from a console application.

Adding a Directmessages Class

We have created a **Directmessage** class in this class we are going to create request and push to RabbitMQ.

First, we have declared Username, Password, and HostName as constant. After that, we have created a method with name **SendMessage** in that message we have created a connection to RabbitMQ server using RabbitMQ.Client after creating connection next we have passed credentials along with HostName to connectionFactory. Next, we have written a simple message **Direct Message** and got it in bytes array form, finally, we are going to assign all these values to a BasicPublish method of **RabbitMQ.Client**

BasicPublish View

```
/// <summary>
/// (Extension method) Convenience overload of BasicPublish.
/// </summary>
/// <remarks>The publication occurs with mandatory=false</remarks>
public static void BasicPublish(this IModel model, string exchange, string routingKey, IBasicProperties basicProperties, byte[] body)
{
    model.BasicPublish(exchange, routingKey, false, basicProperties, body);
}
```

The parameter passed to it

Exchange: **request.exchange**

Routingkey: **directexchange_key**

Code Snippet

```
using RabbitMQ.Client;
using System.Text;

namespace RequestRabbitMQ
{
    public class Directmessages
    {
        private const string UserName = "guest";
        private const string Password = "guest";
        private const string HostName = "localhost";

        public void SendMessage()
        {
            //Main entry point to the RabbitMQ .NET AMQP client
            var connectionFactory = new RabbitMQ.Client.ConnectionFactory()
            {
                UserName = UserName,
                Password = Password,
                HostName = HostName
            };

            var connection = connectionFactory.CreateConnection();
            var model = connection.CreateModel();

            var properties = model.CreateBasicProperties();
            properties.Persistent = false;
```

```
                     byte[] messagebuffer =
Encoding.Default.GetBytes("Direct Message");

            model.BasicPublish("request.exchange",
"directexchange_key", properties, messagebuffer);
            Console.WriteLine("Message Sent");
        }
    }
}
```

Main Code snippet

```
using System;

namespace RequestRabbitMQ
{
    class Program
    {
        static void Main(string[] args)
        {
            Directmessages directmessages = new Directmessages();
            directmessages.SendMessage();
            Console.ReadLine();
        }
    }
}
```

After completing entire process let's save the application and run, after running the application you will see a message on console window as "message sent" just for notification.

After sending message now let's have a look on queue (**request.queue**).

Now Let's See queue status request.queue

If you see Queues status you will see **Ready "1"** which means we have successfully published a message to **request.queue**.

Queues

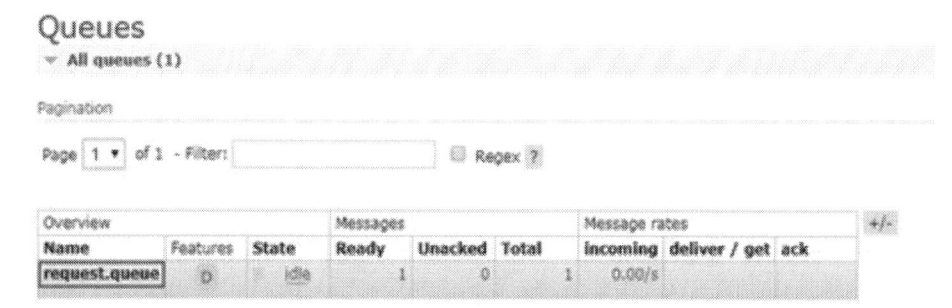

After publishing message next we are going to create .Net Console application for consuming message from queue.

Creating RabbitMQConsumer Application

Let's create another console application for consuming messages from a queue with the Name **RabbitMQConsumer**.

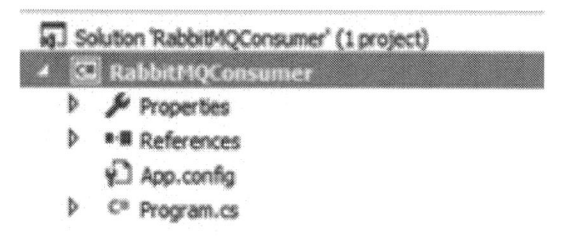

After creating application, we are going to add **RabbitMQ.Client** NuGet package.

Adding RabbitMQ.Client NuGet Package

In this part for creating a connection with RabbitMQ server to create request, we need to add **RabbitMQ.Client** package from NuGet Package.
Command to install: Install-Package **RabbitMQ.Client -Version 5.1.0**

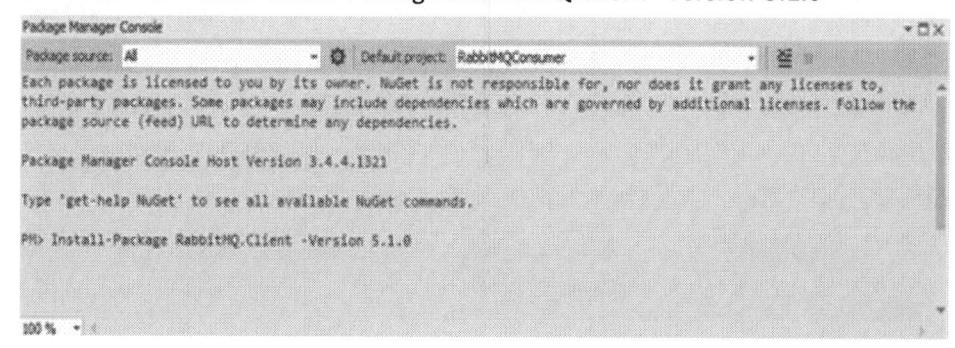

After installing RabbitMQ.Client, we are going to add a class with name

MessageReceiver.

Code snippet of MessageReceiver class

In this part, we have created **MessageReceiver** class and this class inherits **DefaultBasicConsumer** class which is from **RabbitMQ.Client** next we have to override **HandleBasicDeliver** method, this method receives message body next, we are going to write these messages as we can see in its console.

```
using System;
using System.Text;
using RabbitMQ.Client;

namespace RabbitMQConsumer
{
    public class MessageReceiver : DefaultBasicConsumer
    {
        private readonly IModel _channel;

        public MessageReceiver(IModel channel)
        {
            _channel = channel;
        }

        public override void HandleBasicDeliver(string consumerTag, ulong deliveryTag, bool redelivered, string exchange, string routingKey, IBasicProperties properties, byte[] body)
        {
            Console.WriteLine($"Consuming Message");
            Console.WriteLine(string.Concat("Message received from the exchange ", exchange));
            Console.WriteLine(string.Concat("Consumer tag: ", consumerTag));
            Console.WriteLine(string.Concat("Delivery tag: ", deliveryTag));
            Console.WriteLine(string.Concat("Routing tag: ", routingKey));
            Console.WriteLine(string.Concat("Message: ", Encoding.UTF8.GetString(body)));
            _channel.BasicAck(deliveryTag, false);
        }
    }
}
```

After completing understanding code snippet of MessageReceiver class, we are going to call this class in the main method.

Code snippet of main method

In the main method we have created **connectionFactory** class and passed credentials and Hostname, after that we have created connection, next we have created channel and set prefetchCount to 1 such that it tells RabbitMQ not to give more than one message to a worker at a time, Next, we have created an instance of **MessageReceiver** class and passed IModel (channel) to it, in final step we have called **BasicConsume** method and passed queue name to it "**request.queue**" along with this we have set autoAck to false and passed the messageReceiver instance to it.

```
using System;
using System.Collections.Generic;
using System.Linq;
using System.Text;
using System.Threading.Tasks;
using RabbitMQ.Client;

namespace RabbitMQConsumer
{
    class Program
    {
        private const string UserName = "guest";
        private const string Password = "guest";
        private const string HostName = "localhost";

        static void Main(string[] args)
        {
            ConnectionFactory connectionFactory = new ConnectionFactory
            {
                HostName = HostName,
                UserName = UserName,
                Password = Password,
            };

            var connection = connectionFactory.CreateConnection();
            var channel = connection.CreateModel();

            // accept only one unack-ed message at a time
            // uint prefetchSize, ushort prefetchCount, bool global

            channel.BasicQos(0, 1, false);
```

```csharp
                    MessageReceiver messageReceiver = new 
MessageReceiver(channel);
                    channel.BasicConsume("request.queue", false, 
messageReceiver);

                    Console.ReadLine();
            }
        }
    }
```

Note: - prefetchCount

To defeat that, we can set the prefetch count with the value of 1. This tells RabbitMQ not to give more than one message to a worker at a time. Or, in other words, don't dispatch a new message to a worker until it has processed and acknowledged the previous one. Instead, it will dispatch it to the next worker that is still free.

Now we have complete working mechanism Let's create request from "**RequestRabbitMQ**" console and consume a message from "**RabbitMQConsumer**" application.

Queue is Empty

Queues

▼ All queues (1)

Pagination

Page 1 ▼ of 1 - Filter: [   ] ☐ Regex ?

Overview			Messages			Message rates			+/-
Name	Features	State	Ready	Unacked	Total	incoming	deliver / get	ack	
request.queue	D	idle	0	0	0	0.00/s	0.00/s	0.00/s	

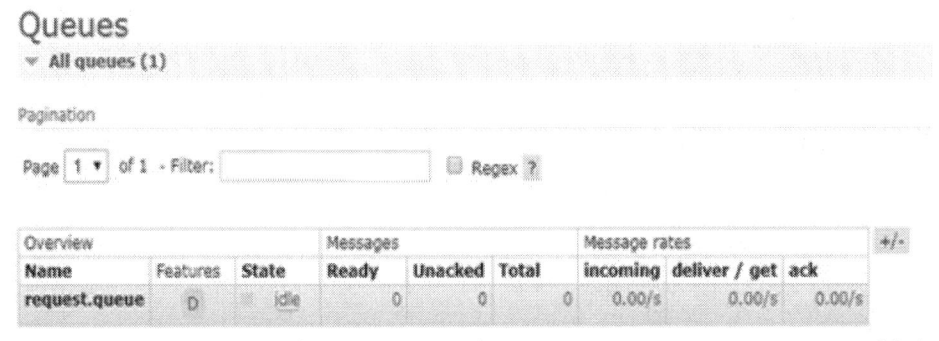

After we saw that queue (request.queue) is empty next we are going to publish message to request.queue.

Publishing Message

```csharp
public class Directmessages
{
    private const string UserName = "guest";
    private const string Password = "guest";
    private const string HostName = "localhost";

    public void SendMessage()
    {
        Code

        byte[] messagebuffer = Encoding.Default.GetBytes("Send My First RabbitMQ Message");

        model.BasicPublish("request.exchange", "directexchange_key", properties, messagebuffer);

        Console.WriteLine("Message Sent");
    }
}
```

After we have published message now let's take a look at (queue) request.queue.

Queue after publishing Message

After we have push message to (queue) request.queue the console application will start consuming it, following is the snapshot:

Consumed Message from request.queue

Finally, we have completed consuming message from RabbitMQ queue.

Conclusion

In this part, we have learned how to Produce and consume RabbitMQ Direct Message Exchanges with .Net Application in step by step way along with that how to connect to RabbitMQ server using **RabbitMQ.Client**, how to create direct exchange, queue and bindings.

Using RabbitMQ Topic Message Exchanges with .Net Application

In this part, we are going to use Topic Message Exchanges and push messages into RabbitMQ using .Net Application and RabbitMQ.Client and read messages from RabbitMQ using .Net Application and RabbitMQ.Client in step by step way.

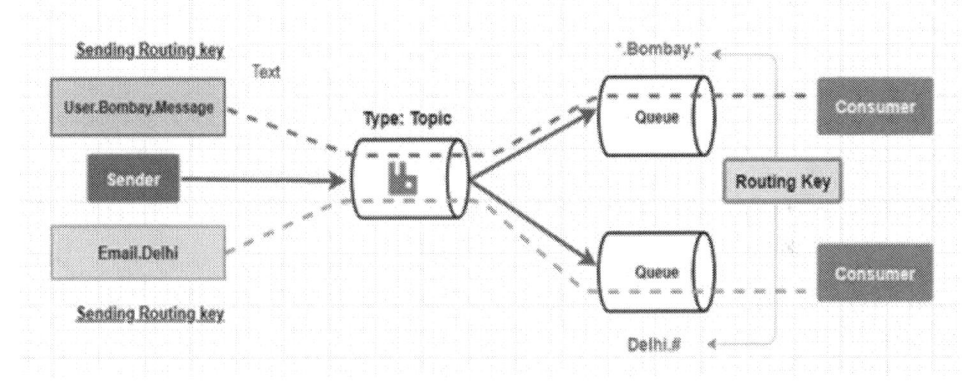

What is the Topic Exchange?

The topic exchange does a wildcard match between the routing key and the routing pattern specified in the binding.

In topic exchange, the routing key must not be a simple text such as *Bombay* it must be words delimited by dots such as "*.bombay.*" or "#.bombay" or "Bombay.#".

For example: I have two queues, one for Bombay and the other for Delhi then the user must send routing key which will match the pattern of routing key, then only that message will be added to queue, else message will be lost.

Note:

* (star) can substitute for exactly one word.

(hash) can substitute for zero or more words.

Creating RequestRabbitMQ Application

Let's create a simple console application with Name **RequestRabbitMQ**.

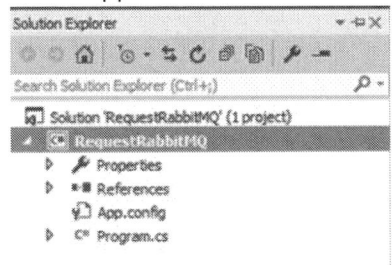

After creating application next we are going to add **RabbitMQ.Client** NuGet package.

Adding RabbitMQ.Client NuGet Package

In this part for creating a connection with the RabbitMQ server to create request, we need to add **RabbitMQ.Client** package from NuGet Package.

Command to install: - Install-Package **RabbitMQ.Client -Version 5.1.0**

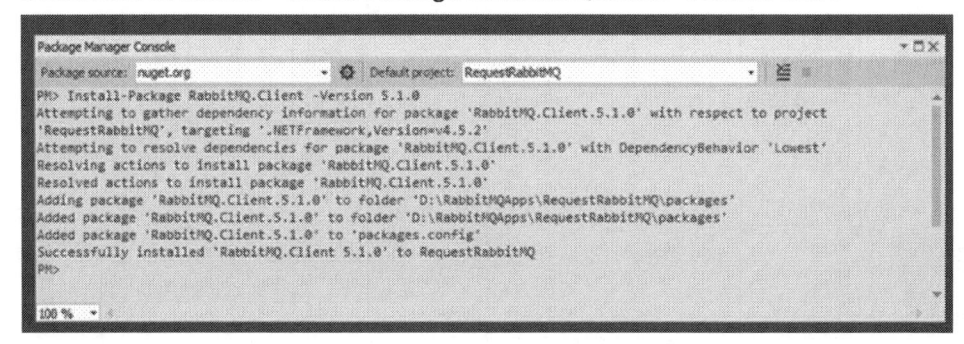

After installing NuGet package of **RabbitMQ.Client** next we are going to create an exchange from web admin console.

Adding Topic Exchange

Go to http://localhost:15672/#/exchanges, name exchange as topic.exchange after entering name, we select Type as topic and click on add exchange button to create.

After adding **topic.exchange** next we are going to Add 2 Queue.

Adding Queue

In this part we are going to create 2 queues with different routing key but for same **topic.exchange**.

Go to http://localhost:15672/#/queues

1. topic.bombay.queue
2. topic.delhi.queue

Adding first queue with name **topic.bombay.queue**.

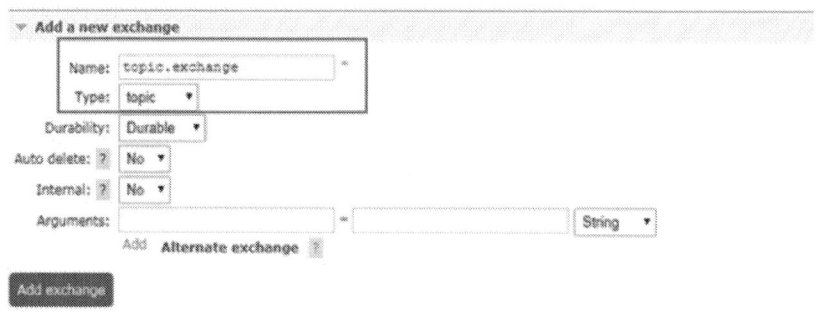

Adding the second queue **topic.delhi.queue**.

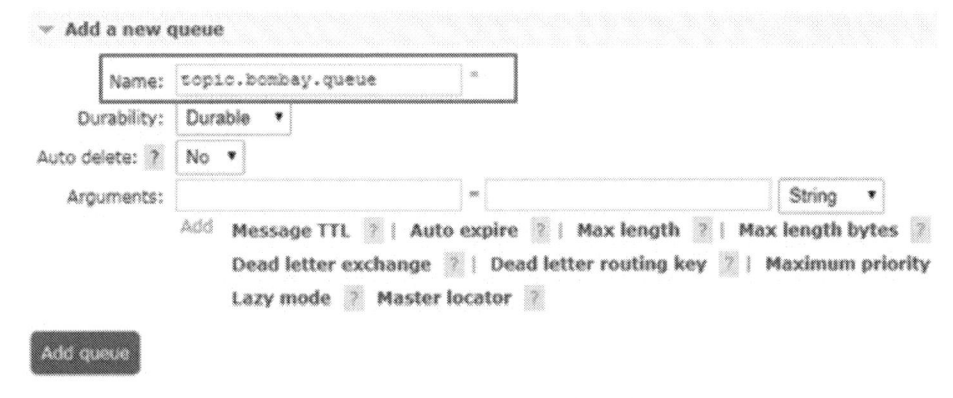

[Screenshot: Add a new queue form with Name: topic.bombay.queue, Durability: Durable, Auto delete: No]

After adding queue, the added queues are displayed.

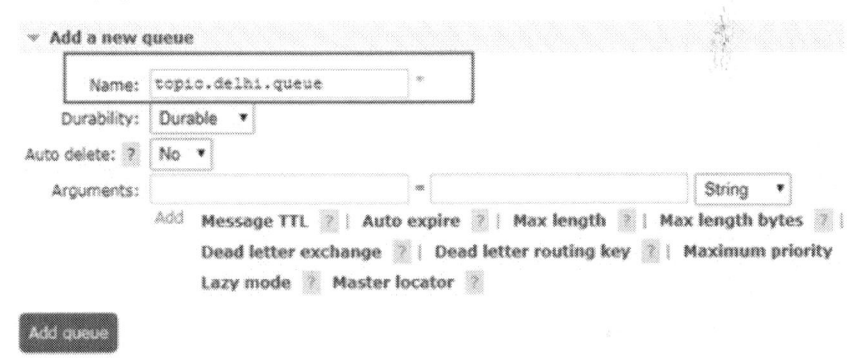

[Screenshot: Add a new queue form with Name: topic.delhi.queue, Durability: Durable, Auto delete: No]

After adding queue, we are going to bind queue with **topic.exchange**.

Binding the topic.bombay.queue with topic.exchange

In this part, we are binding **topic.exchange** with a **topic.bombay.queue** using a pattern of unique routing key "*.Bombay.*".

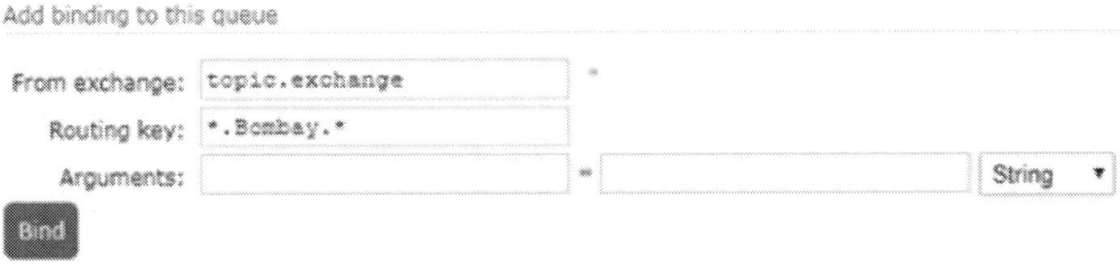

*[Screenshot: Add binding to this queue - From exchange: topic.exchange, Routing key: *.Bombay.*]*

Snapshot of binding

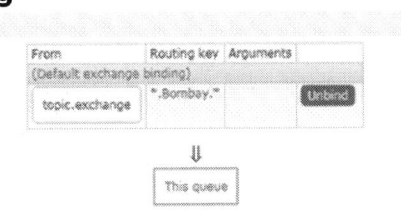

*[Screenshot: Bindings showing From: topic.exchange, Routing key: *.Bombay.*, with Unbind button, pointing to "This queue"]*

Binding the topic.delhi.queue with topic.exchange

In this part, we are binding **topic.exchange** with a **topic.delhi.queue** using a pattern of unique routing key "**Delhi.#**".

Snapshot of Binding

After completing with binding, we are going to publish message.

Adding a Topicmessages Class

We have created a **Topicmessage** class, in this class we are going to create request and push to RabbitMQ.

First, we have declared Username, Password, and HostName as constant. After that, we have created a method with name **SendMessage** in that message we have created a connection to RabbitMQ server using RabbitMQ.Client after creating connection next, we have passed credentials along with HostName to connectionFactory. Next, we have written a simple message **Message from Topic Exchange 'Bombay'** and got it in bytes array form, finally, we are going to assign all these values to a **BasicPublish** method of **RabbitMQ.Client**.

Routing pattern: - "any text .Bombay. any text".

Examples of routing key:

"Order.Bombay.Pizza",

"Book.Bombay.Hotels",

 "Visit.Bombay.Parks",

"List.Bombay.Colleges".

The parameter passed to it

Exchange: "topic.exchange"

Routing key: "Message.Bombay.Email"

Code Snippet

```
    public class Topicmessages
    {
        private const string UserName = "guest";
        private const string Password = "guest";
        private const string HostName = "localhost";

        public void SendMessage()
        {
            //Main entry point to the RabbitMQ .NET AMQP client
            var connectionFactory = new RabbitMQ.Client.ConnectionFactory()
            {
                UserName = UserName, Password = Password, HostName = HostName
            };

            var connection = connectionFactory.CreateConnection();
            var model = connection.CreateModel();
            var properties = model.CreateBasicProperties();
            properties.Persistent = false;

            byte[] messagebuffer = Encoding.Default.GetBytes("Message from Topic Exchange 'Bombay' ");
            model.BasicPublish("topic.exchange", "Message.Bombay.Email", properties, messagebuffer);
            Console.WriteLine("Message Sent From :- topic.exchange ");
            Console.WriteLine("Routing Key :- Message.Bombay.Email");
            Console.WriteLine("Message Sent");
        }
    }
```

Main Code snippet

```
using System;
namespace RequestRabbitMQ
{
```

```
    class Program
    {
        static void Main(string[] args)
        {
                Topicmessages topicmessages = new 
Topicmessages();
            topicmessages.SendMessage();
            Console.ReadLine();
        }
    }
}
```

After completing the entire process let's save the application and run, after running the application you will see a message on console window as "Message sent" just for notification, it means we have successfully published a message to queue of "topic.bombay.queue".

Published Message to "topic.bombay.queue"

```
Message Sent From :- topic.exchange
Routing Key :- Message.Bombay.Email
Message Sent
```

Now Let's See queue status "request.queue"

If you see Queues status, you will see **Ready "1"** which means we have successfully published a message to **topic.bombay.queue**.

Overview			Messages			Message rates			+/-
Name	Features	State	Ready	Unacked	Total	incoming	deliver / get	ack	
request.queue	D	idle	0	0	0				
topic.bombay.queue	D	idle	1	0	1	0.00/s	0.00/s	0.00/s	
topic.delhi.queue	D	idle	0	0	0				

After publishing a message, next we are going to create .Net Console application for consuming message from the queue.

Creating RabbitMQConsumer Application

Let's create another console application for consuming messages from a queue **RabbitMQConsumer**.

Learning RabbitMQ With C#

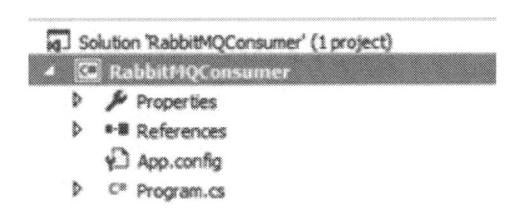

After creating application, we are going to add **RabbitMQ.Client** NuGet package.

Adding RabbitMQ.Client NuGet Package

In this part for creating a connection with the RabbitMQ server to create request, we need to add **RabbitMQ.Client** package from NuGet Package.

Command to install: Install-Package **RabbitMQ.Client -Version 5.1.0**

After installing **RabbitMQ.Client**, we are going to add a class **MessageReceiver**.

Code snippet of MessageReceiver class

In this part, we have created **MessageReceiver** class and this class inherits **DefaultBasicConsumer** class which is from **RabbitMQ.Client** next we have to override HandleBasicDeliver method, this method receives message body next, we are going to write these messages as we can see in its console.

```
public class MessageReceiver : DefaultBasicConsumer
    {
        private readonly IModel _channel;

        public MessageReceiver(IModel channel)
        {
            _channel = channel;
        }

        public override void HandleBasicDeliver(string consumerTag, ulong deliveryTag, bool redelivered, string exchange, string routingKey, IBasicProperties properties, byte[] body)
        {
```

```csharp
            Console.WriteLine($"Consuming Topic Message");
                    Console.WriteLine(string.Concat("Message received from the exchange ", exchange));
                    Console.WriteLine(string.Concat("Consumer tag: ", consumerTag));
                    Console.WriteLine(string.Concat("Delivery tag: ", deliveryTag));
                    Console.WriteLine(string.Concat("Routing tag: ", routingKey));
                    Console.WriteLine(string.Concat("Message: ", Encoding.UTF8.GetString(body)));
                    _channel.BasicAck(deliveryTag, false);
            }
        }
```

After completing with understanding the code snippet of **MessageReceiver** class next we are going to call this class in the Main method.

Code snippet of Main Method while consuming "topic.bombay.queue"

In the main method we have created **connectionFactory** class and passed credentials and Hostname after that we have created connection, next we have created channel and set prefetchCount to 1 such that it tells RabbitMQ not to give more than one message to a worker at a time, Next, we have created instance of **MessageReceiver** class and passed IModel (channel) to it, in final step we have called **BasicConsume** method and passed queue name to it "**topic.bombay.queue**" along with this, we have set autoAck to false and passed the **messageReceiver** instance to it.

```csharp
using System;
using RabbitMQ.Client;

namespace RabbitMQConsumer
{
    class Program
    {
        private const string UserName = "guest";
        private const string Password = "guest";
        private const string HostName = "localhost";

        static void Main(string[] args)
        {
            ConnectionFactory connectionFactory = new ConnectionFactory
            {
                HostName = HostName,
```

```csharp
                UserName = UserName,
                Password = Password,
            };

                                var connection =
connectionFactory.CreateConnection();
            var channel = connection.CreateModel();

            // accept only one unack-ed message at a time
            // uint prefetchSize, ushort prefetchCount, bool global

            channel.BasicQos(0, 1, false);

            // ==== prefetchCount
            // In order to defeat that we can set the prefetch count with the value of 1
            // This tells RabbitMQ not to give more than one message to a worker at a time.
                    // Or, in other words, don't dispatch a new message to a worker until it has
                    // processed and acknowledged the previous one. Instead, it will dispatch it to t
                    // the next worker that is not still busy.

                    MessageReceiver messageReceiver = new MessageReceiver(channel);
            channel.BasicConsume("topic.bombay.queue", false, messageReceiver);

            Console.ReadLine();
        }
    }
}
```

Now we have complete working mechanism. Let's create request from **RequestRabbitMQ** console and consume a message from "**RabbitMQConsumer**" application.

The queue has one Request which we have published

The following snapshot contains only one message in **topic.bombay.queue** which we have published.

Queues

▼ All queues (3)

Pagination

Page 1 ▼ of 1 - Filter: [   ] ☐ Regex ?

Overview			Messages			Message rates			+/-
Name	Features	State	Ready	Unacked	Total	incoming	deliver / get	ack	
request.queue	D	idle	0	0	0				
topic.bombay.queue	D	idle	1	0	1	0.00/s	0.00/s	0.00/s	
topic.delhi.queue	D	idle	0	0	0				

Consumed Message from topic.bombay.queue

```
Consuming Topic Message
Message received from the exchange topic.exchange
Consumer tag: amq.ctag-tfp1bon4gcnoF401N-RiQA
Delivery tag: 1
Routing tag: Message.Bombay.Email
Message: Message from Topic Exchange 'Bombay'
```

After successfully consuming message from **topic.bombay.queue,** we are going to publish a message to another queue which is **topic.delhi.queue**.

Published Message to topic.delhi.queue

In **topicmessage** class, I have just made a small change in routing key **Delhi.TicketBooking** and message which we send to publish a message to **topic.delhi.queue**.

Routing pattern: "Delhi. any text"

Examples of routing key: "Delhi.Pizza", "Delhi.Hotels", "Delhi.Parks", "Delhi.Colleges"

Code Snippet

```csharp
public class Topicmessages
    {
        private const string UserName = "guest";
        private const string Password = "guest";
        private const string HostName = "localhost";

        public void SendMessage()
        {
            //Main entry point to the RabbitMQ .NET AMQP client
            var connectionFactory = new
```

```csharp
RabbitMQ.Client.ConnectionFactory()
    {
        UserName = UserName,
        Password = Password,
        HostName = HostName
    };

                    var connection = connectionFactory.CreateConnection();
    var model = connection.CreateModel();

    var properties = model.CreateBasicProperties();
    properties.Persistent = false;

    byte[] messagebuffer = Encoding.Default.GetBytes
        ("Message from Topic Exchange 'Delhi' ");

            model.BasicPublish("topic.exchange",
"Delhi.TicketBooking",
        properties, messagebuffer);

        Console.WriteLine("Message Sent From :- topic.exchange ");
        Console.WriteLine("Routing Key :- Delhi.TicketBooking");
        Console.WriteLine("Message Sent");
    }
}
```

After making changes let's save and run application to publish message to **topic.delhi.queue**.

Published Message to "topic.delhi.queue"

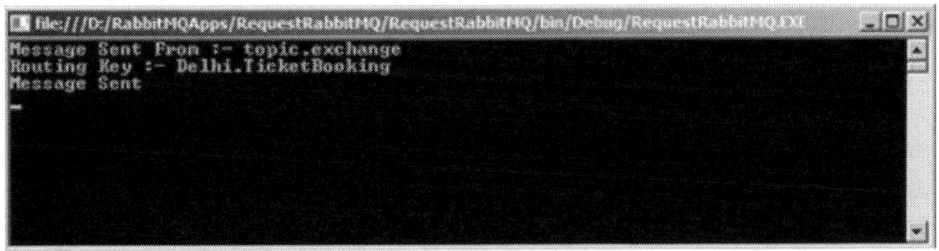

```
Message Sent From :- topic.exchange
Routing Key :- Delhi.TicketBooking
Message Sent
```

The queue has one request which we have published

Queues

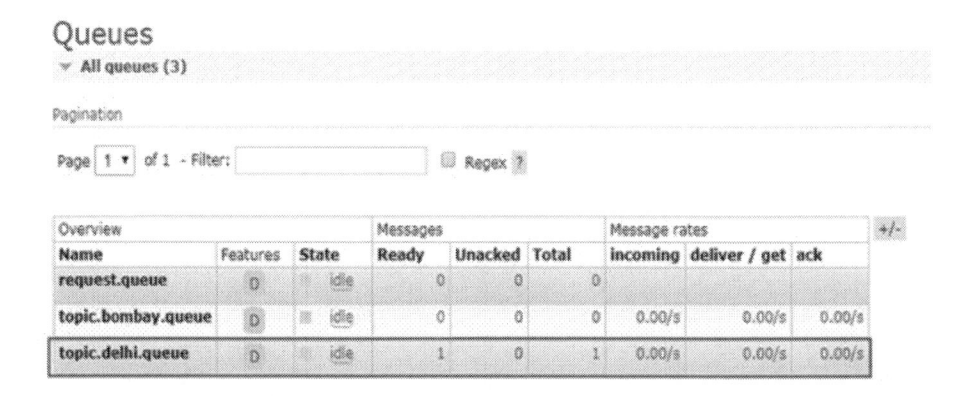

▼ All queues (3)

Pagination

Page 1 ▼ of 1 - Filter: [   ] ☐ Regex ?

Overview				Messages			Message rates			+/-
Name	Features		State	Ready	Unacked	Total	incoming	deliver / get	ack	
request.queue	D		idle	0	0	0				
topic.bombay.queue	D		idle	0	0	0	0.00/s	0.00/s	0.00/s	
topic.delhi.queue	D		idle	1	0	1	0.00/s	0.00/s	0.00/s	

Code snippet of Main Method while consuming "topic.delhi.queue" from RabbitMQConsumer

In this part, I have just changed the queue name to **topic.delhi.queue** in RabbitMQConsumer application.

```
using System;
using RabbitMQ.Client;

namespace RabbitMQConsumer
{
    class Program
    {
        private const string UserName = "guest";
        private const string Password = "guest";
        private const string HostName = "localhost";

        static void Main(string[] args)
        {
            ConnectionFactory connectionFactory = new ConnectionFactory
            {
                HostName = HostName,
                UserName = UserName,
                Password = Password,
            };

            var connection = connectionFactory.CreateConnection();
            var channel = connection.CreateModel();

            // accept only one unack-ed message at a time
            // uint prefetchSize, ushort prefetchCount, bool
```

global

```
        channel.BasicQos(0, 1, false);

        // ==== prefetchCount
        // In order to defeat that we can set the prefetch count with the value of 1
        // This tells RabbitMQ not to give more than one message to a worker at a time.
        // Or, in other words, don't dispatch a new message to a worker until it has
        // processed and acknowledged the previous one. Instead, it will dispatch it to t
        // the next worker that is not still busy.

            MessageReceiver messageReceiver = new MessageReceiver(channel);
        channel.BasicConsume("topic.delhi.queue", false, messageReceiver);
        Console.ReadLine();
      }
    }
}
```

Consumed Message from topic.delhi.queue

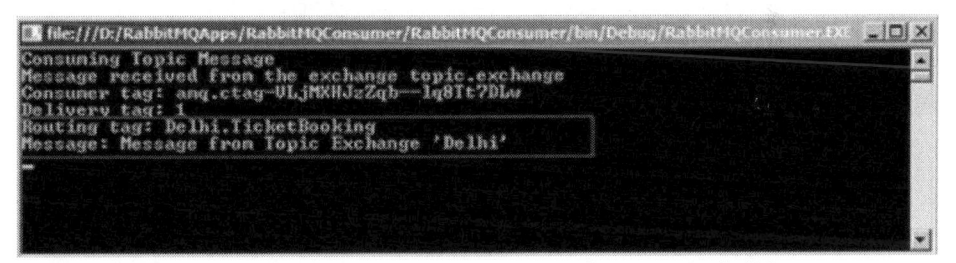

Finally, we have completed consuming message from **topic.delhi.queue** queue.

Conclusion

In this part, we have learned how to use Topic Message Exchanges and how to create exchange and queue for topic exchange and how to push messages into RabbitMQ using .Net Application and RabbitMQ.Client and read messages from RabbitMQ using .Net Application and RabbitMQ.Client in step by step way.

Using RabbitMQ Fanout Message Exchanges with .Net Application

In this part, we are going to use Fanout Message Exchanges and push messages into RabbitMQ using .Net Application and RabbitMQ.Client and read messages from RabbitMQ using .Net Application and RabbitMQ.Client in step by step way.

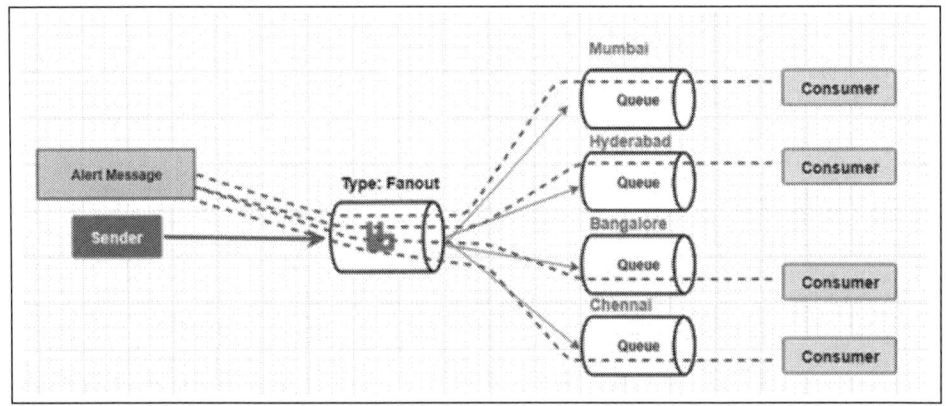

What is a Fanout Exchange?

A fanout exchange routes messages to all of the queues that are bound to it.

This exchange is used when you want to publish a common message to all queue which is connected to the particular exchange and in fanout exchange **routing key** is ignored.

For example, if a company has updated some guidelines and you want to push the guideline to all branches, at that time you can use fanout exchange.

Creating RequestRabbitMQ Application

Let's Create a simple console application with **RequestRabbitMQ**.

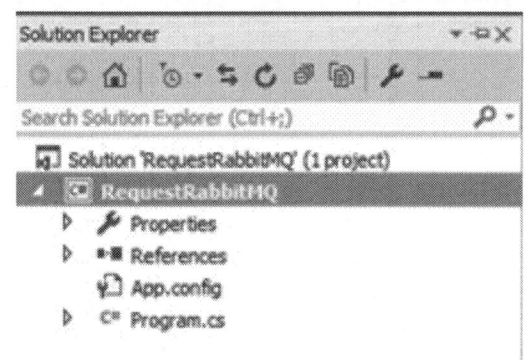

After creating application, we are going to add **RabbitMQ.Client** NuGet package.

Adding RabbitMQ.Client NuGet Package

In this part for creating a connection with the RabbitMQ server to create request, we need to add **RabbitMQ.Client** package from NuGet Package.

Command to install: - **Install-Package RabbitMQ.Client -Version 5.1.0**

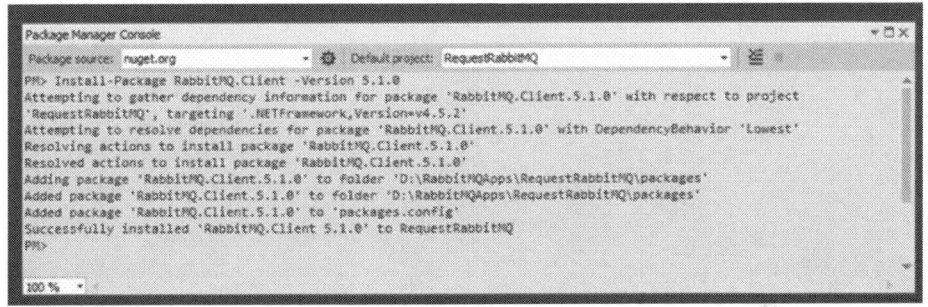

After installing NuGet package of **RabbitMQ.Client** next we are going to create an exchange from web admin console.

Adding Fanout Exchange

Go to http://localhost:15672/#/exchanges, name exchange as fanout.exchange after entering name, we select Type as "fanout" and click on add exchange button to create.

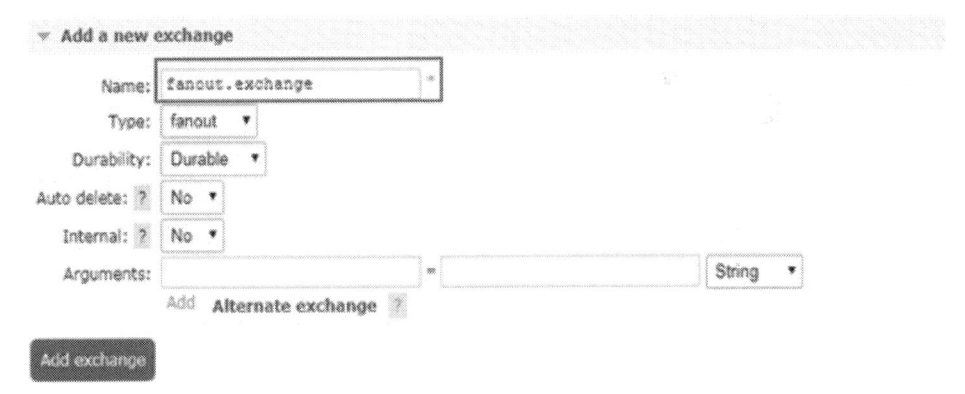

After adding **fanout.exchange** next we are going to Add 4 Queue and bind it to same exchange.

Adding Queue

In this part we are going to create 4 queues with different routing key but for same **fanout.exchange**.

Go to http://localhost:15672/#/queues

1. Mumbai
2. Hyderabad
3. Bangalore

4. Chennai

Adding the first queue with name **Mumbai**.

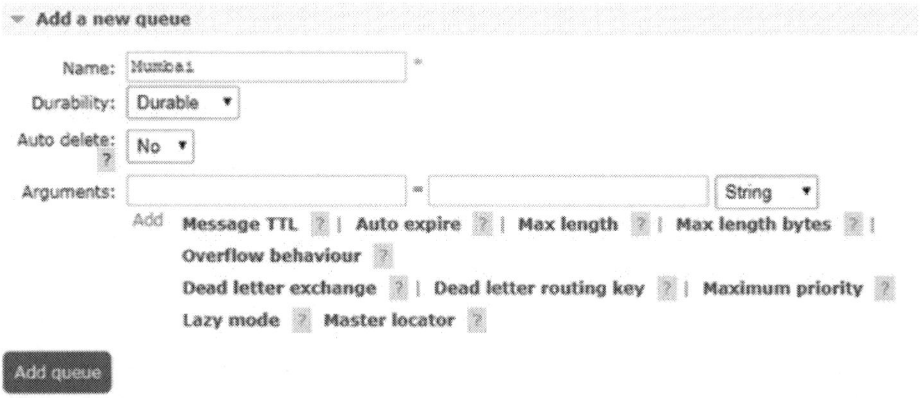

In a similar way, I have added rest of queues as shown in the following snapshot.

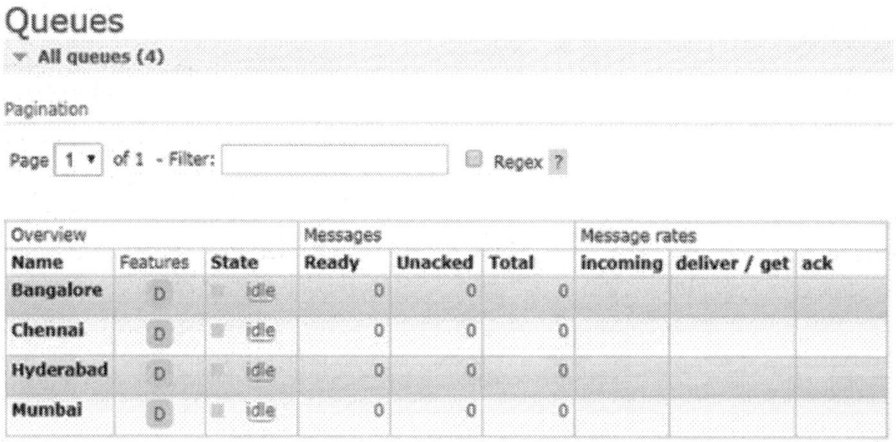

After adding all queues, we are going to bind queues with **fanout.exchange**.

Binding the Queues (Bangalore, Chennai, Hyderabad, Mumbai) with fanout.exchange

In this part, we are binding **fanout.exchange** with all queues (Bangalore, Chennai, Hyderabad, Mumbai).

First queue that we are going to bind is Bangalore.

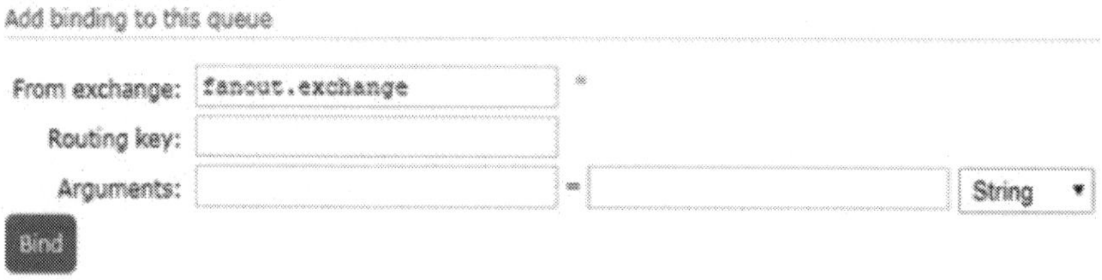

Snapshot of Binding

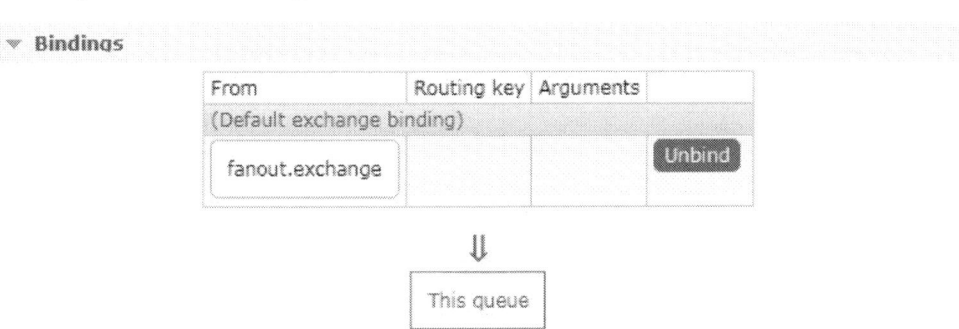

▼ Bindings

From	Routing key	Arguments	
(Default exchange binding)			
fanout.exchange			Unbind

⇓

This queue

An example is for Bangalore queue, in a similar way we are going to do for all rest of queues which are there of fanout exchange (Chennai, Hyderabad, Mumbai).

After completing with binding, we are going to publish message.

Adding a Fanoutmessages Class

We have created a **fanoutmessage** class, in this class we are going to create request and push to RabbitMQ.

First, we have declared Username, Password and HostName as constant. After that, we have created a method with name **SendMessage** in that message we have created a connection to RabbitMQ server using RabbitMQ.Client after creating connection next, we have passed credentials along with HostName to connectionFactory. Next, we have written a simple message **Message is of fanout Exchange type** and got it in bytes array form, finally, we are going to assign all these values to a BasicPublish method of **RabbitMQ.Client**

While assigning we are going to set exchange as **fanout.exchange** and there will not be routing key for fanout exchange.

Code Snippet

```
using System;
using RabbitMQ.Client;
using System.Text;

namespace RequestRabbitMQ
{
    public class Fanoutmessages
    {
        private const string UserName = "guest";
        private const string Password = "guest";
        private const string HostName = "localhost";

        public void SendMessage()
```

```csharp
        {
            //Main entry point to the RabbitMQ .NET AMQP client
            var connectionFactory = new RabbitMQ.Client.ConnectionFactory()
            {
                UserName = UserName,
                Password = Password,
                HostName = HostName
            };

            var connection = connectionFactory.CreateConnection();
            var model = connection.CreateModel();

            var properties = model.CreateBasicProperties();
            properties.Persistent = false;


            byte[] messagebuffer = Encoding.Default.GetBytes("Message is of fanout Exchange type");
            model.BasicPublish("fanout.exchange", "", properties, messagebuffer);
            Console.WriteLine("Message Sent From :- fanout.exchange ");
            Console.WriteLine("Routing Key :-  Routing key is Not required for fanout exchange");
            Console.WriteLine("Message Sent");
        }
    }
}
```

Main Code snippet

```csharp
using System;
namespace RequestRabbitMQ
{
    class Program
    {
        static void Main(string[] args)
        {
            Fanoutmessages fanoutmessages = new Fanoutmessages();
            fanoutmessages.SendMessage();
            Console.ReadLine();
        }
    }
}
```

After completing the entire process let's save the application and run, after running the application you will see a message on console window as "Message sent" just for notification it means we have successfully published a message to all queues of "fanout.exchange" exchange.

Published Message to all queues of "fanout.exchange"

```
Message Sent From :- fanout.exchange
Routing Key :-  Routing key is Not required for fanout exchange
Message Sent
```

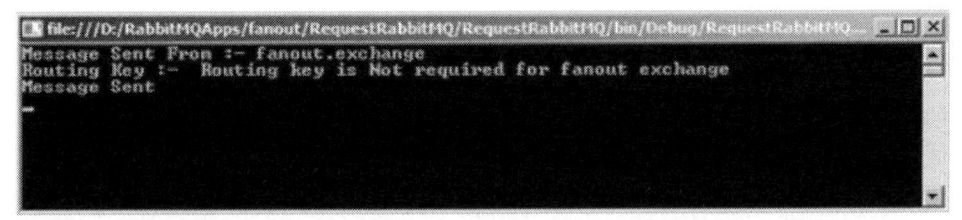

Now let's see queue status (Bangalore, Chennai, Hyderabad, Mumbai) queue

If you see Queues status you will see **Ready "1"** which means we have successfully published a message to all queues of fanout exchanges.

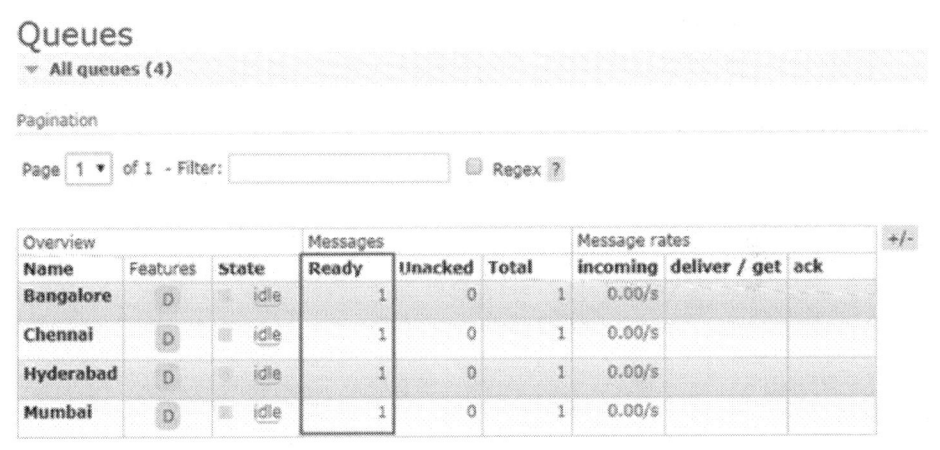

Queues

All queues (4)

Pagination

Page 1 ▼ of 1 - Filter: [   ] ☐ Regex ?

Overview			Messages			Message rates			+/-
Name	Features	State	Ready	Unacked	Total	incoming	deliver / get	ack	
Bangalore	D	idle	1	0	1	0.00/s			
Chennai	D	idle	1	0	1	0.00/s			
Hyderabad	D	idle	1	0	1	0.00/s			
Mumbai	D	idle	1	0	1	0.00/s			

After publishing a message next we are going to create .Net Console application for consuming message from the queue.

Creating RabbitMQConsumer Application

Let's create another console application for consuming messages from a queue **RabbitMQConsumer**.

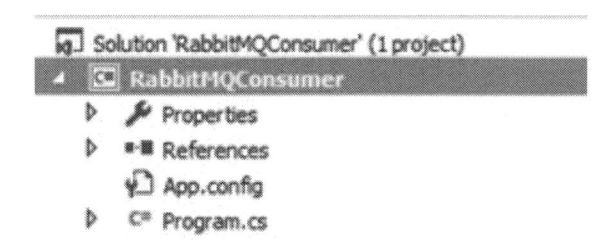

After creating application, we are going to add **RabbitMQ.Client** NuGet package.

Adding RabbitMQ.Client NuGet Package

In this part for creating a connection with the RabbitMQ server to create request, we need to add **RabbitMQ.Client** package from NuGet package.
Command to install: **Install-Package RabbitMQ.Client -Version 5.1.0**

After installing **RabbitMQ.Client** next we are going to add a class with name **MessageReceiver**.

Code snippet of MessageReceiver class

In this part, we have created **MessageReceiver** class and this class inherits **DefaultBasicConsumer** class which is from **RabbitMQ.Client** next we have to override **HandleBasicDeliver** method this method receives message body next, we are going to write these messages as we can see in its console.

```
    public class MessageReceiver : DefaultBasicConsumer
        {
            private readonly IModel _channel;

            public MessageReceiver(IModel channel)
            {
                _channel = channel;
            }

            public override void HandleBasicDeliver(string consumerTag, ulong deliveryTag, bool redelivered, string exchange, string routingKey, IBasicProperties properties,
```

```csharp
byte[] body)
        {
            Console.WriteLine($"Consuming fanout Message");
            Console.WriteLine(string.Concat("Message received from the exchange ", exchange));
            Console.WriteLine(string.Concat("Consumer tag: ", consumerTag));
            Console.WriteLine(string.Concat("Delivery tag: ", deliveryTag));
            Console.WriteLine(string.Concat("Routing tag: ", routingKey));
            Console.WriteLine(string.Concat("Message: ", Encoding.UTF8.GetString(body)));
            _channel.BasicAck(deliveryTag, false);
        }
    }
```

After completing with understanding code snippet of **MessageReceiver** class next we are going to call this class in the main method.

Code snippet of Main Method while consuming "Mumbai" queue

In the main method we have created **connectionFactory** class and passed credentials and Hostname after that we have created connection, next we have created channel and set prefetchCount to 1 such that it tells RabbitMQ not to give more than one message to a worker at a time. Next, we have created instance of **MessageReceiver** class and passed IModel (channel) to it, in final step we have called **BasicConsume** method and passed queue name to it "**Mumbai**" along with this we have set autoAck to false and passed the **messageReceiver** instance to it.

```csharp
// uint prefetchSize, ushort prefetchCount, bool global
channel.BasicQos(0, 1, false);

// ==== prefetchCount
// In order to defeat that we can set the prefetch count with the value of 1
// This tells RabbitMQ not to give more than one message to a worker at a time.
// Or, in other words, don't dispatch a new message to a worker until it has
// processed and acknowledged the previous one. Instead, it will dispatch it to t
// he next worker that is not still busy.

MessageReceiver messageReceiver = new MessageReceiver(channel);
channel.BasicConsume("Mumbai", false, messageReceiver);

Console.ReadLine();
}
```

```csharp
using System;
using RabbitMQ.Client;
namespace RabbitMQConsumer
{
    class Program
```

```csharp
    {
        private const string UserName = "guest";
        private const string Password = "guest";
        private const string HostName = "localhost";

        static void Main(string[] args)
        {
            ConnectionFactory connectionFactory = new ConnectionFactory
            {
                HostName = HostName,
                UserName = UserName,
                Password = Password,
            };

            var connection = connectionFactory.CreateConnection();
            var channel = connection.CreateModel();
            // accept only one unack-ed message at a time
            // uint prefetchSize, ushort prefetchCount, bool global

            channel.BasicQos(0, 1, false);
            // ==== prefetchCount
            // In order to defeat that we can set the prefetch count with the value of 1
            // This tells RabbitMQ not to give more than one message to a worker at a time.
            // Or, in other words, don't dispatch a new message to a worker until it has
            // processed and acknowledged the previous one. Instead, it will dispatch it to t
            // the next worker that is not still busy.
            MessageReceiver messageReceiver = new MessageReceiver(channel);
            channel.BasicConsume("Mumbai", false, messageReceiver);

            Console.ReadLine();
        }
    }
}
```

Learning RabbitMQ With C#

Now, we have complete working mechanism. Let's create request from **RequestRabbitMQ** console and consume a message from **RabbitMQConsumer** application.

The queue has one Request which we have published

The below snapshot shows all queues have one message which we have published using fanout exchange.

Queues
▼ All queues (4)

Pagination

Page 1 ▼ of 1 - Filter: [   ] ☐ Regex ?

Overview			Messages			Message rates			+/-
Name	Features	State	Ready	Unacked	Total	incoming	deliver / get	ack	
Bangalore	D	idle	1	0	1	0.00/s			
Chennai	D	idle	1	0	1	0.00/s			
Hyderabad	D	idle	1	0	1	0.00/s			
Mumbai	D	idle	1	0	1	0.00/s			

Consumed Message from Mumbai queue

This message is only consumed from Mumbai queue, rest of the queues are unread till now.

```
file:///D:/RabbitMQApps/fanout/RabbitMQConsumer/RabbitMQConsumer/bin/Debug/RabbitMQConsu...
Consuming fanout Message from Mumbai
Message received from the exchange fanout.exchange
Consumer tag: amq.ctag-rYWjTDJmz_GSC-3mk3D8fA
Delivery tag: 1
Routing tag:
Message: Message is of fanout Exchange type
```

The status of the queue after reading Message from Mumbai queue.

Overview			Messages			Message rates			+/-
Name	Features	State	Ready	Unacked	Total	incoming	deliver / get	ack	
Bangalore	D	idle	1	0	1	0.00/s			
Chennai	D	idle	1	0	1	0.00/s			
Hyderabad	D	idle	1	0	1	0.00/s			
Mumbai	D	idle	0	0	0	0.00/s	0.00/s	0.00/s	

In a similar way, if we read a message from Bangalore queue than just need to make a change in "**queue name**" in **RabbitMQConsumer**.

Consumed Message from Bangalore queue

We have just changed the name of the queue from Mumbai to Bangalore. To read a message from Bangalore queue.

```
using System;
using RabbitMQ.Client;

namespace RabbitMQConsumer
{
    class Program
    {
        private const string UserName = "guest";
        private const string Password = "guest";
        private const string HostName = "localhost";

        static void Main(string[] args)
        {
            ConnectionFactory connectionFactory = new ConnectionFactory
            {
                HostName = HostName,
                UserName = UserName,
                Password = Password,
            };

            var connection = connectionFactory.CreateConnection();
            var channel = connection.CreateModel();

            // accept only one unack-ed message at a time
            // uint prefetchSize, ushort prefetchCount, bool global

            channel.BasicQos(0, 1, false);

            #region MyRegion
            // ==== prefetchCount
            // In order to defeat that we can set the prefetch count with the value of 1
            // This tells RabbitMQ not to give more than one message to a worker at a time.
            // Or, in other words, don't dispatch a new message to a worker until it has
            // processed and acknowledged the previous one.
```

```
                Instead, it will dispatch it to t
                        // the next worker that is not still busy.
                        #endregion

                            MessageReceiver messageReceiver = new
MessageReceiver(channel);
                            channel.BasicConsume("Bangalore", false,
messageReceiver);

                        Console.ReadLine();
            }
        }
}
```

Let's save and run application to red message from Bangalore queue.

The status of the queue after reading Message from Bangalore queue.

Overview			Messages			Message rates			+/-
Name	Features	State	Ready	Unacked	Total	incoming	deliver / get	ack	
Bangalore	D	idle	0	0	0	0.00/s	0.00/s	0.00/s	
Chennai	D	idle	1	0	1	0.00/s			
Hyderabad	D	idle	1	0	1	0.00/s			
Mumbai	D	idle	0	0	0	0.00/s	0.00/s	0.00/s	

Finally, we have learned how fanout exchange works and how we can publish messages and consume messages from fanout exchange in step by step way.

Conclusion

In this part, we have learned how to use Fanout Message Exchanges and how to create exchange and queue for Fanout exchange and how to push messages into RabbitMQ using .Net Application and RabbitMQ.Client and read messages from RabbitMQ using .Net Application and RabbitMQ.Client in step by step way.

Using RabbitMQ Headers Message Exchanges with .Net Application

In this part, we are going to use Headers Message Exchanges and push messages into RabbitMQ using .Net Application and RabbitMQ.Client and read messages from RabbitMQ using .Net Application and RabbitMQ.Client in step by step way.

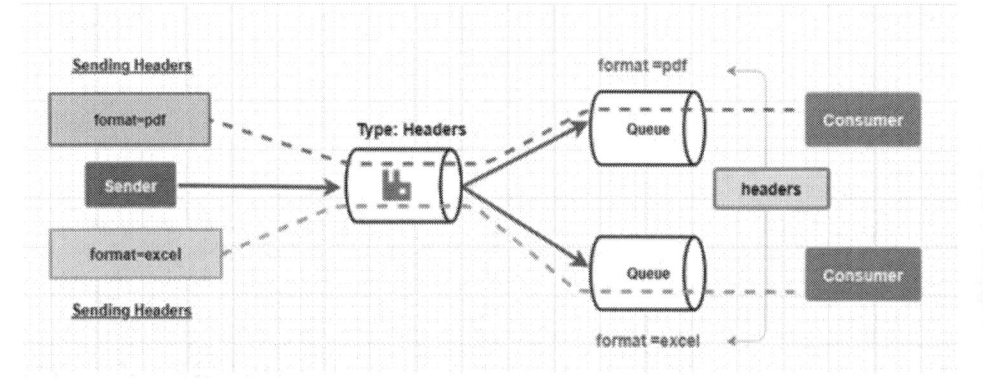

What is a Headers exchange?

Headers exchanges use the message header attributes for routing.

This exchange is used when you want to send a message to queue but this time it will not depend on routing key it will be sent to queue on the basis of header attributes.

Creating RequestRabbitMQ Application

Let's create a simple console application with Name "**RequestRabbitMQ**".

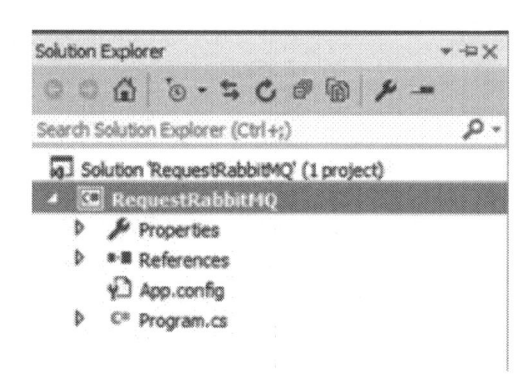

After creating application, we are going to add "**RabbitMQ.Client**" NuGet package.

Adding RabbitMQ.Client NuGet Package

In this part for creating a connection with the RabbitMQ server to create request, we need to add **RabbitMQ.Client** package from NuGet Package.

Command to install: **Install-Package RabbitMQ.Client -Version 5.1.0**

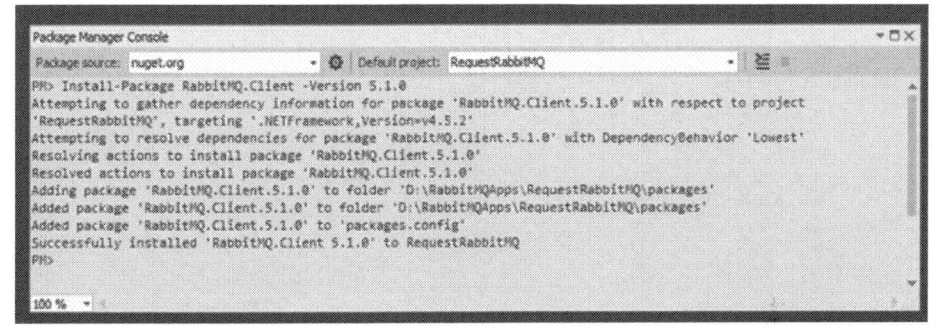

After installing NuGet package of "**RabbitMQ.Client**" next we are going to create an exchange from web admin console.

Note:

Headers exchange routes message based on header values instead of routing keys.

A special argument named x-match has 2 values {all, any} where all is the default value of a headers binding.

− x-match = all : means that all the values must match

− x-match = any : means just one matching header value is sufficient

Referenced from: http://javasampleapproach.com/spring-framework/spring-boot/springboot-rabbitmq-headers-exchange

Adding Fanout Exchange

Go to http://localhost:15672/#/exchanges, name exchange as headers.exchange after entering name, we select Type as "headers" and click on add exchange button to create.

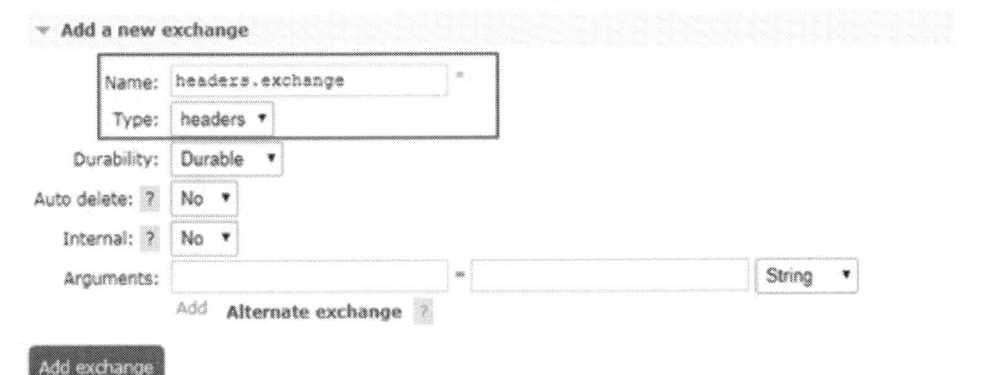

After adding "**headers.exchange**" next we are going to Add two Queue and bind it to same exchange.

Adding queue

In this part, we are going to create two queues without different routing key but for same "**headers.exchange**".

Go to http://localhost:15672/#/queues:

1. ReportPDF
2. ReportExcel

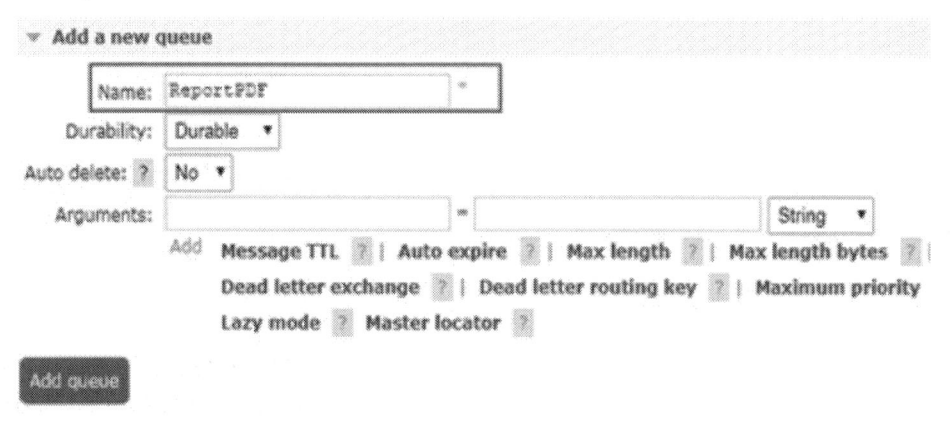

In a similar way, I have added rest of queues as shown in the following snapshot.

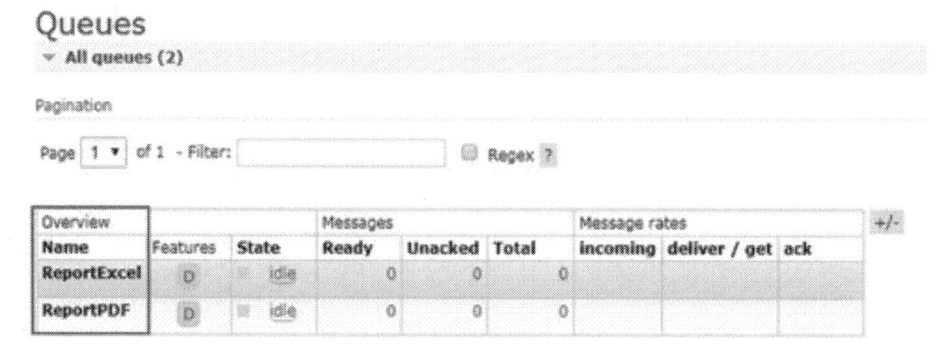

After adding all the queues, we are going to bind queues with "**headers.exchange**".

Binding the Queues

In this part, we are binding **headers.exchange** with a "**ReportPDF**" queue and while binding we are going to set arguments such as format=pdf and x-match=all these arguments need to be passed by producer in the header such that message will be sent to the accurate queue.

Snapshot of Binding

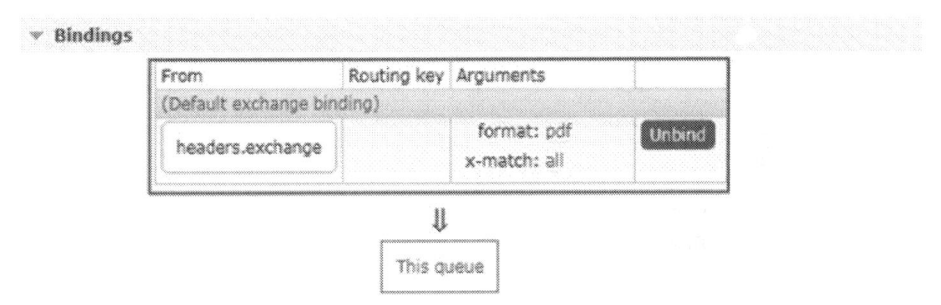

In this part, we are binding **headers.exchange** with a "**ReportExcel**" queue and while binding we are going to set arguments such as format=pdf and x-match=all this argument needs to be passed by producer in the header such that message will be sent to the accurate queue.

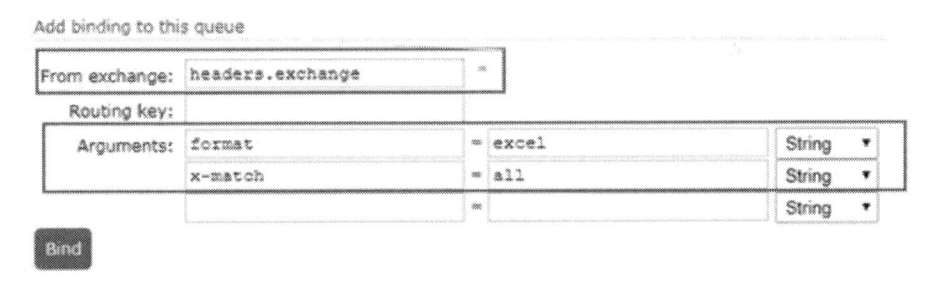

Snapshot of Binding

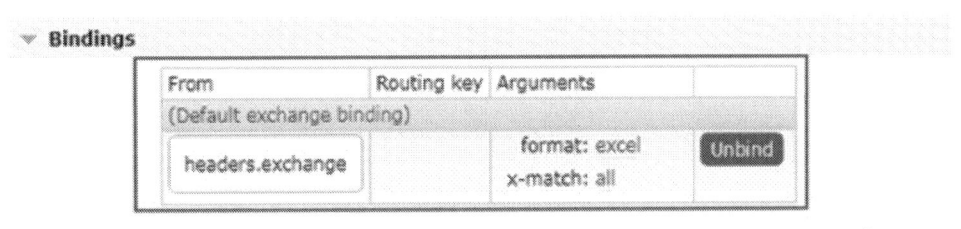

After binding all arguments to their respective queue, next we are going to publish the message for that we are going to add a class.

Adding a Headersmessages Class

We have created a **Headersmessages** class, in this class we are going to create request and push to RabbitMQ.

First, we have declared Username, Password, and HostName as constant. After that, we have created a method with name "**SendMessage**" in that message we have created a connection to RabbitMQ server using RabbitMQ.Client after creating connection next we have passed credentials along with HostName to connectionFactory. Next, we have written a simple message **Message to Headers Exchange 'format=pdf'** and got it in bytes array form, finally, we are going assign all these values to a BasicPublish method of "**RabbitMQ.Client**"

While assigning we are going to set exchange as "**headers.exchange**" and there will not be routing key for headers exchange.

Code Snippet

```
public class Headersmessages
    {
        private const string UserName = "guest";
        private const string Password = "guest";
        private const string HostName = "localhost";

        public void SendMessage()
        {
            //Main entry point to the RabbitMQ .NET AMQP client
            var connectionFactory = new RabbitMQ.Client.ConnectionFactory()
            {
                UserName = UserName,
                Password = Password,
                HostName = HostName
            };

            var connection = connectionFactory.CreateConnection();
            var model = connection.CreateModel();

            var properties = model.CreateBasicProperties();
            properties.Persistent = false;

            Dictionary<string,object> dictionary = new Dictionary<string, object>();
            dictionary.Add("format", "pdf");
            properties.Headers = dictionary;
```

```
                         byte[] messagebuffer =
Encoding.Default.GetBytes("Message to Headers
        Exchange 'format=pdf' ");

            model.BasicPublish("headers.exchange", "",
properties, messagebuffer);

            Console.WriteLine("Message Sent From :-
headers.exchange ");
            Console.WriteLine("Routing Key :- Does not need
routing key");
            Console.WriteLine("Message Sent");
        }
    }
```

Main Code snippet

```
using System;
namespace RequestRabbitMQ
{
    class Program
    {
        static void Main(string[] args)
        {
            Headersmessages headersmessages = new
Headersmessages();
            headersmessages.SendMessage();
            Console.ReadLine();
        }
    }
}
```

After completing the entire process, let's save the application and run after running the application you will see a message on console window as "Message sent" just for notification it means we have successfully published a message to queue of "headers. exchange".

Published Message to Reportpdf queues of "Headers.exchange"

```
Message Sent From :- headers.exchange
Routing Key :- Does not need routing key
Message Sent
```

Now let's see queue status

If you see queues status of Reportpdf queue you will see **Ready "1"** which means, we have successfully published a message to Reportpdf queues using headers exchanges.

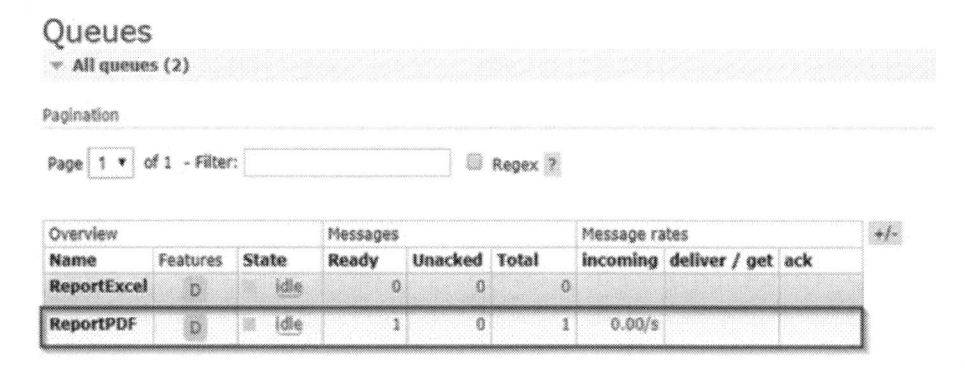

Overview			Messages			Message rates			+/-
Name	Features	State	Ready	Unacked	Total	incoming	deliver / get	ack	
ReportExcel	D	idle	0	0	0				
ReportPDF	D	idle	1	0	1	0.00/s			

After publishing a message next, we are going to create .Net Console application for consuming message from the queue.

Creating RabbitMQConsumer Application

Let's create another console application for consuming messages from a queue with **RabbitMQConsumer**.

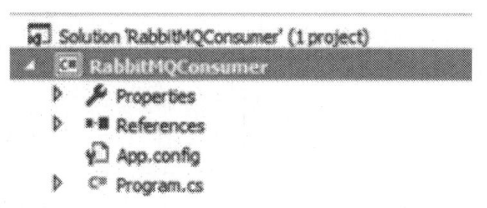

After creating application, we are going to add **RabbitMQ.Client** NuGet package.

Adding RabbitMQ.Client NuGet Package

In this part for creating a connection with the RabbitMQ server to create request, we need to add **RabbitMQ.Client** package from NuGet Package.

Command to install: **Install-Package RabbitMQ.Client -Version 5.1.0**

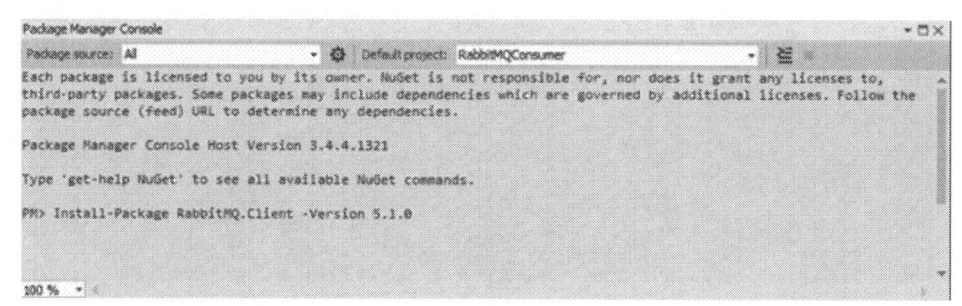

Learning RabbitMQ With C#

After installing **RabbitMQ.Client**, we are going to add a class with name "**MessageReceiver**".

Code snippet of MessageReceiver class

In this part, we have created **MessageReceiver** class and this class inherits **DefaultBasicConsumer** class which is from **RabbitMQ.Client** next we have to override **HandleBasicDeliver** method, this method receives message body next, we are going to write these messages as we can see in its console.

```csharp
using System;
using System.Text;
using RabbitMQ.Client;

namespace RabbitMQConsumer
{
    public class MessageReceiver : DefaultBasicConsumer
    {
        private readonly IModel _channel;

        public MessageReceiver(IModel channel)
        {
            _channel = channel;
        }

        public override void HandleBasicDeliver(string consumerTag, ulong deliveryTag, bool redelivered, string exchange, string routingKey, IBasicProperties properties, byte[] body)
        {
            Console.WriteLine($"Consuming Headers Message");
            Console.WriteLine(string.Concat("Message received from the exchange ", exchange));
            Console.WriteLine(string.Concat("Consumer tag: ", consumerTag));
            Console.WriteLine(string.Concat("Delivery tag: ", deliveryTag));
            Console.WriteLine(string.Concat("Routing tag: ", routingKey));
            Console.WriteLine(string.Concat("Message: ", Encoding.UTF8.GetString(body)));
            _channel.BasicAck(deliveryTag, false);
        }
    }
}
```

After completing with understanding code snippet of **MessageReceiver** class next we are going to call this class in the main method.

Code snippet of main method while consuming "Mumbai" queue

In the main method we have created **connectionFactory** class and passed credentials and Hostname after that we have created connection, next we have created channel and set **prefetchCount** to 1 such that it tells RabbitMQ not to give more than one message to a worker at a time. Next, we have created instance of **MessageReceiver** class and passed IModel (channel) to it, in final step we have called "**BasicConsume**" method and passed queue name to it "**ReportPDF**" along with this we have set autoAck to false and passed the **messageReceiver** instance to it.

```
channel.BasicQos(0, 1, false);

// ==== prefetchCount
// In order to defeat that we can set the prefetch count with the value of 1
// This tells RabbitMQ not to give more than one message to a worker at a time.
// Or, in other words, don't dispatch a new message to a worker until it has
// processed and acknowledged the previous one. Instead, it will dispatch it to t
// he next worker that is not still busy.

MessageReceiver messageReceiver = new MessageReceiver(channel);
channel.BasicConsume("ReportPDF", false, messageReceiver);

Console.ReadLine();
```

```csharp
using System;
using RabbitMQ.Client;

namespace RabbitMQConsumer
{
    class Program
    {
        private const string UserName = "guest";
        private const string Password = "guest";
        private const string HostName = "localhost";

        static void Main(string[] args)
        {
            ConnectionFactory connectionFactory = new ConnectionFactory
            {
                HostName = HostName,
                UserName = UserName,
                Password = Password,
            };
            var connection = connectionFactory.CreateConnection();
```

```csharp
            var channel = connection.CreateModel();

            // accept only one unack-ed message at a time
            // uint prefetchSize, ushort prefetchCount, bool global

            channel.BasicQos(0, 1, false);

            // ==== prefetchCount
            // In order to defeat that we can set the prefetch count with the value of 1
            // This tells RabbitMQ not to give more than one message to a worker at a time.
            // Or, in other words, don't dispatch a new message to a worker until it has
            // processed and acknowledged the previous one. Instead, it will dispatch it to t
            // the next worker that is not still busy.

            MessageReceiver messageReceiver = new MessageReceiver(channel);
            channel.BasicConsume("ReportPDF", false, messageReceiver);

            Console.ReadLine();
        }
    }
}
```

Now we have completed with consuming module. Let's consume a message from "**ReportPDF**" queue which we have already published.

The queue has one request which we have published

The following snapshot shows of ReportPDF queue have one message which we have published using headers exchange.

Queues

▼ All queues (2)

Pagination

Page 1 ▼ of 1 - Filter: [   ]   ☐ Regex ?

Overview			Messages			Message rates			+/-
Name	Features	State	Ready	Unacked	Total	incoming	deliver / get	ack	
ReportExcel	D	idle	0	0	0				
ReportPDF	D	idle	1	0	1	0.00/s			

Consumed Message from ReportPDF queue

The snapshot while consuming message is only consumed from ReportPDF queue.

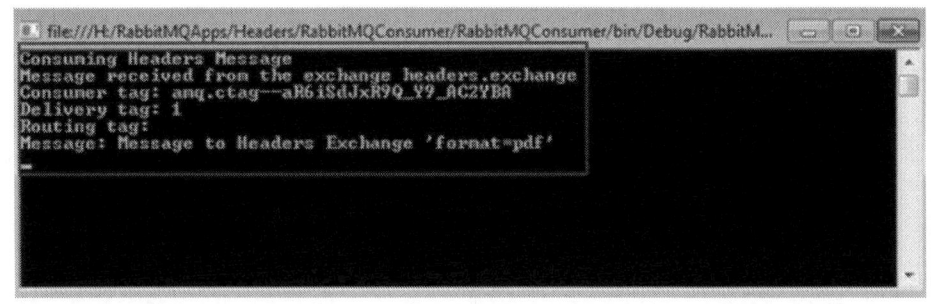

```
Consuming Headers Message
Message received from the exchange headers.exchange
Consumer tag: amq.ctag--aR6iSdJxR9Q_Y9_AC2YBA
Delivery tag: 1
Routing tag:
Message: Message to Headers Exchange 'format=pdf'
```

The status of the queue after reading message from ReportPDF queue.

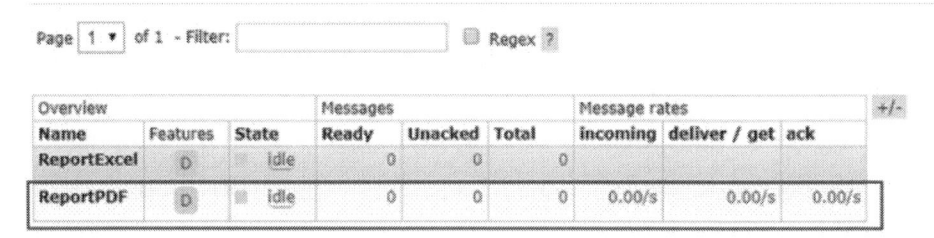

Overview			Messages			Message rates			+/-
Name	Features	State	Ready	Unacked	Total	incoming	deliver / get	ack	
ReportExcel	D	idle	0	0	0				
ReportPDF	D	idle	0	0	0	0.00/s	0.00/s	0.00/s	

We have completed consuming messages from ReportPDF queue.

Conclusion

In this part, we have learned how to use headers Message Exchanges and how to create exchange and queue for headers exchange and how to push messages into RabbitMQ using .Net Application and RabbitMQ.Client and read messages from RabbitMQ using .Net Application and RabbitMQ.Client in step by step way.

Manufactured by Amazon.ca
Bolton, ON